THE STEP-BY-STEP SEWING GUIDE

CUSHIONS, CURTAINS & BLINDS

THE STEP-BY-STEP SEWING GUIDE

CUSHIONS, CURTAINS & BLINDS

Introduced by Carolyn Watts

Macdonald Orbis

Acknowledgments

The artwork was drawn by the following artists: Lindsay Blow, Sharon Finmark, Eugene Fleury, Susanna Lisle, Jill Shipley and Sara Silcock.

The photographs on the following pages are by courtesy of: Camera Press 22, 23, 43, 77, 79; Coloroll 65; Curtain Net Advisory Bureau 31, 32, 36, 80; Dulux 90; Laura Ashley 68, 85; Mayfair 37; Rufflette 38-9, 46, 57; Sanderson 33, 58; Swish 63, 67, 73.

The remaining photographs were taken by the following photographers: Jan Baldwin, Tom Belshaw, Jon Bouchier, Alan Bramley, Clive Helm, Spike Powell and Jerry Tubby.

Front cover: Camera Press
Half title page: Tom Belshaw
Title page: Laura Ashley
Back cover: Jon Bouchier

A Macdonald Orbis BOOK

First published in Great Britain by
Orbis Publishing Limited, London 1986

Reprinted in 1987 by
Macdonald & Co (Publishers) Ltd
London & Sydney

A member of BPCC plc

This material previously appeared in the partwork
SuperStitch

Printed in Italy.

ISBN: 0 356 15179 4

Macdonald & Co (Publishers) Ltd
Greater London House
Hampstead Road
London NW1 7QX

Contents

Introduction

Most soft furnishings were originally developed out of necessity – cushions to make chairs more comfortable, curtains to keep out draughts, blinds to cut out light. But the desire to be different and to embellish and style in one's own way takes over – and transforms an object of necessity into one of decor. These days it seems we more than ever want our homes to look good. We are demanding more individuality – less of the 'off the peg' products. We want to create our own surroundings and, not only that, we want to create a uniqueness that sets us apart – to sew something special that is the mark of our style.

Cushions, curtains, blinds: these are the things in home-furnishing terms that count for so much. A well-made, well-draped set of curtains, a distinctive roller blind or a collection of co-ordinated cushions are the elements that can complete a room, adding softness, colour and pattern, emphasising shape or transforming a colour scheme.

Cushions, Curtains and Blinds provides you with comprehensive instructions, taking you through each project step-by-step, showing the basics and giving ideas for finishing touches and a truly personal look. Whether you're a thoroughly skilled needlewoman or a complete beginner, the projects are simple to follow, give guidelines for calculating fabric quantities and are illustrated throughout with diagrams and photographs.

Cushions are perhaps the most likely contenders for a first sewing project because they are so quick and easy to make up and because they use only relatively small quantities of fabric. Starting with the simplest of square, rectangular and round cushion-covers with hand-sewn openings, the cushion-making chapters progress through cushions with fancy, frilled edges to those with gussets for added depth, and to giant sizes in the form of floor cushions and sag bags.

Cushions, whether plain or gusseted, are the cheapest soft furnishings to make in terms of the amount of fabric and sewing required. They are, therefore, one of the most popular 'accessory' items – used to add a splash of colour or pattern or to 'soften' the looks and feel of a sofa or chair. With the addition of a gusset or frill, a cushion instantly looks more sumptuous and expensive and the gusset, as well as making the cushion deeper, can also be used to show off shape. Contrasting piping in the seams or a co-ordinating or toning fabric as a frill or a gusset can give another opportunity to introduce an individual look. Floor cushions and sag-bag cushions have great fun value. Cheaper by far than conventional seating, they are ideal for children or for situations where shortage of space makes sofas or chairs impractical.

Daunted by the prospect of tackling what they believe to be a difficult project, many people fight shy of making curtains and blinds. But a successful result actually hinges on accurate measuring and cutting. In fact, as a sewing exercise making curtains is particularly easy. Remember, you are dealing with straight seams and there are no tricky techniques involved. This makes curtain sewing a whole lot easier than dressmaking!

As with any new venture, if you're uneasy about launching into curtain making, start with something simple. Unlined curtains are so straightforward: a seam down each side, a bottom hem and a heading tape or casing at the top. And, if you are wondering how to calculate fabric quantities, what sort of effect the different types of heading tape give and how much tape you'll need – all these vital points are covered in full detail in the curtain chapters. Having mastered the art of unlined curtains, detachable linings will seem easy, and from there it is only one step forward to sewn-in curtain linings.

The chapters on curtain pelmets, valances, borders and tie-backs show how little extras can be added to achieve the 'designer look'. Here is your chance to give your curtains an individual stamp – to show your own style. The shape of a pelmet, the trim on a valance, the matching of curtain border to tie-back – these are the small details that decide your decorative style. You'll find extensive examples, instruction, inspiration and plenty of scope to develop and adapt your own ideas. Additional chapters extend curtains' original function to cover café and shower curtains, explaining how you can put your curtain-making skills to use in these specialised fields.

Following the same principle of starting with the simplest, a plain roller blind makes an excellent first project, and if you can use a pre-stiffened blind fabric, there is only the minimum of sewing involved. Austrian, Roman and festooned blinds are based on the same sewing structure, and although the extensive gathering or folding of the fabric may look like a complex conglomeration of special sewing techniques, they are in fact surprisingly straight-forward to make up. The gathering or folding is created by an arrangement of tape and cords sewn on to the back of the blind.

In the realm of soft furnishings, it is almost impossible to 'go over the top' – to create too much. The natural draping qualities of a fabric, its softness to the touch and lack of harsh defining lines, make it a perfect candidate for indulgence. Don't be afraid to create more than pure function dictates. Give cushions contrasting frills for a bold effect, use a blind in addition to curtains at a window, add a pelmet or valance to show off curtains.

Modern furnishing trends favour co-ordinating fabrics that are colour matched and pattern co-ordinated to allow for mixing and matching. Often marketed as total collections, these fabrics are easy to put together – saving time looking for a particular matching fabric and money by avoiding an expensive wrong choice.

It is my hope that, with the help of all the exciting fabrics available today, we shall now see soft furnishings in a new light. That we come to treat soft furnishings in the same way as we do clothes and fashion, that we pay more attention to style and design – so that our homes become as much part of our character as the clothes we wear. I hope this book will help you to see that the road to individuality and style is through sewing something special yourself and that *Cushions, Curtains and Blinds* will become your starting point and inspiration.

Carolyn Watts, 1986

Cushions for comfort

*Cushions are just about the most versatile of home furnishings.
They provide a splash of colour, tone or contrast,
and give added comfort to a sofa or chair. Once you have
learned how to make the basic cushion shapes, you
can add frills, piping or fancy borders for a decorative effect.*

To make a simple cushion cover all you need is a front, a back, and a method for opening and closing. Before you set to work with the scissors cutting out the fabric, decide on the type of opening you want to use, as this determines the cutting measurements.

A zip, Velcro or overlap opening is the most satisfactory type if you're likely to be laundering the cushion cover frequently, because this makes the cushion pad easy to take out and put back.

A hand sewn opening, although easier to make in the first place, needs to be carefully unpicked and resewn each time the pad is removed.

Choose any furnishing fabric to make up a cushion cover. You can create a bold show mixing style, colour and pattern by buying up fabric remnants or, if you're sewing curtains, loose covers and other furnishings for your home, use left overs from cutting out the fabric to make co-ordinating covers at no extra cost.

The cushion cover itself is sewn to fit over a cushion pad. Never put fillings straight into your cushion cover. All filling has to be enclosed in its own inner cover to give a cushion pad that can be removed from the cushion cover for laundering.

Re-use the pads you've got already if they're still in good condition. If you're buying a new pad, manufactured cushion pads are available in a large number of sizes and shapes, square, rectangular and round, so you should be able to find one with the dimensions to suit your needs.

Right: Cushions in a mixture of shapes and sizes add subtle touches of colour to this cool grey living room.

Making square and rectangular cushion covers

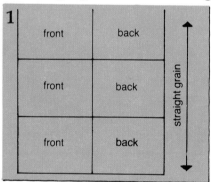

Measuring and cutting

Use a tape measure to size up your cushion pad. It's important to measure right over the pad to take account of its padded out shape. Measure in both directions to find the size of the square or rectangle you will need for the cover and to these measurements add 1.5cm/⅝in seam allowance all round. For a plump-looking cushion, do not add seam allowance so that, after you

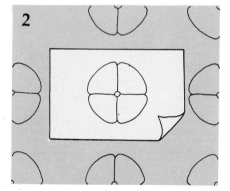

have sewn the cover together, it fits tightly over the pad.

For each cushion cover, cut a front and a back piece (two sections for the back piece if you've chosen to have a back zip opening, page 11). Lay the fabric on a flat surface and with a ruler and tailor's chalk mark up the sizes of the squares or rectangles.

1 Mark all the squares/rectangles on the straight grain of the fabric with the pattern (if applicable) running in the same direction.

If the fabric has a definite bold pattern, place this centrally on the cushion cover for best effect. To do this, cut a piece of tracing paper to the size of your square/rectangle.

2 Place the tracing paper pattern on the fabric, centring over the main design.

When you're cutting several covers from the same fabric, it helps to estimate the total amount of fabric if you draw up a plan first. On a small piece of paper, mark up the width of your fabric and then draw on, with measurements, the number of fabric pieces needed. Make sure that the combined measurements across the width come close to, but do not exceed, the width of your fabric. To estimate the total length of fabric you will need, simply add up the measurements of the pieces marked down the length.

Hand-sewn side opening This is the simplest of cushion covers to make, its only disadvantage is that you have to resew the opening when the cover is cleaned.

Right sides facing, tack the two pieces of fabric round three sides 1.5cm/⅝in from outer edge with a 90° right angle at each corner. On a rectangular cover, leave a short side untacked. To give rounded corners tack a curve instead of a right angle at each corner. After sewing, trim fabric and notch almost to the seamline.

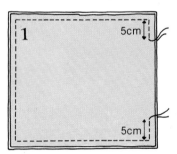

1 On the untacked side, tack 5cm/2in of the seam from both ends, leaving the centre of the seam open. Sew all seams with a 1.5cm/⅝in seam allowance leaving the untacked sections open.

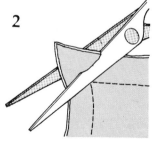

2 On each corner, cut the seam allowance diagonally close to the stitching to reduce bulk. Neaten the raw edges by zigzagging on a sewing machine.

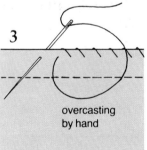

3 Alternatively overcast by hand to neaten. Turn to right side and add the cushion pad. Tack the opening closed. Handstitch opening with slip stitches. Remove tacking.

9

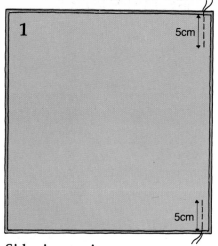

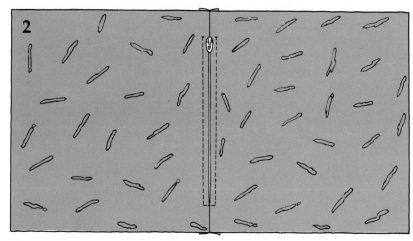

Side zip opening

Lay the two squares/rectangles right sides facing.

1 On one side (short side for a rectangle) tack together for 5cm/2in from each corner along seam allowance. Sew. Remove tacking. Press these short seams flat and press seam allowance to wrong side between the sewn seams. Lay the zip, which should be the same size as the opening, face up on a flat surface and with wrong side of fabric to zip, place open section of seam over the zip teeth. Tack zip in place.

2 On the right side of the fabric, sew down both sides of the zip and across the bottom close to the teeth using the zipper foot on your machine, or as close to the teeth as you can get with the normal sewing foot. Remove tacking. Open the zip and with right sides of the two pieces of fabric facing, tack and sew round the other three sides. Remove tacking. Neaten raw edges. Turn to right side.

Other opening methods In place of a zip you can use a length of press stud tape or Velcro. Make up cover in the same way as for a hand-sewn side opening. Place tape or Velcro on either side of the opening and slip stitch or machine in place.

Making round cushion covers

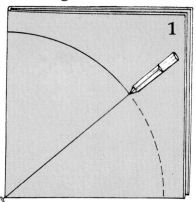

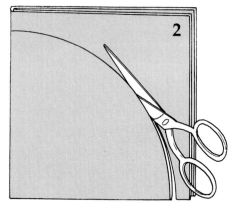

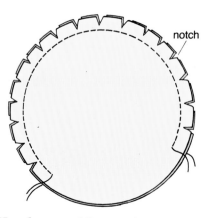

notch

Measuring and cutting

The success of a round cover depends on cutting a perfect circle from the fabric. Measure across the diameter of your cushion pad and add 3cm/1¼in (1.5cm/⅝in seam allowance each side). Cut a square of paper slightly largely than the diameter plus seam allowance.

1 Fold this paper square into four sections. Tie a length of string securely round a pencil and cut this off to half the diameter of the cushion plus 1.5cm/⅝in seam allowance. Again for a plump cushion do not add the seam allowance, and you will get a snug fit. Lay the folded paper on a board and pin the loose end of the string to the point of the folded corner with a drawing pin.

Hold the pencil upright and, at full extent of the string, mark the paper with the pencil in a curve.

2 Take out drawing pin and cut along the curve through all four layers of the paper. Open out the paper and you will have a perfect circle.

This circular paper pattern can be made up in tracing paper if you want to see through the pattern to centre it over a fabric design.

Cut two circles of fabric for each cover. A different pattern has to be made for the back of the cover, if you are placing a zip in the back (right).

Hand-sewn side opening

This is the easiest of round cushion covers to make up, as there is no fastening. However, the opening will have to be unpicked and re-sewn each time for washing.

Right sides facing, lay the two circles of fabric together and tack round the circumference with a 1.5cm/⅝in seam allowance, leaving an opening sufficient to squeeze in cushion pad. Sew. Remove tacking. Notch into the seam allowance all round (except the opening) close to stitching line. Turn cover through to right side and add cushion pad. Tack opening closed and slip stitch by hand. Remove tacking.

Creative cushion covers

Once you're familiar with the basic cushion-making skills, you can think more creatively in design terms. Always remember to sew on any motifs or decoration *before* assembling the cushion pieces. As a taster, the ideas (shown right) are simple and effective.

Simple machine patchwork is marvellously quick and uses up odd scraps of fabric.

Ribbons can be sewn on in a plaid design or as a decorative border.

Cotton lace, backed by a piece of taffeta in a contrasting colour, looks pretty for a bedroom.

Appliquéd motifs are fun to make up. As a short cut, you can cut out a motif from left-over curtain material. A fabric with a regular pattern or printed with squares, diamonds or stripes is easy to quilt and makes a soft padded cushion cover.

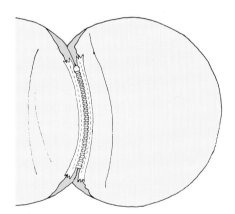

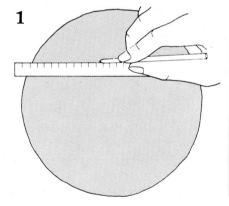

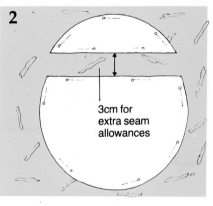

3cm for extra seam allowances

Side zip opening

Choose a zip long enough to take the pad. Pin the two circles together right sides facing, leaving an opening in the seam allowance the length of the zip. Tack along the seam allowance for 2.5cm/1in either side of the opening. Sew. Remove tacking and pins. Press short seams flat. Pin the zip into the opening between the stitched seams. This seam is on the curve, so ease the fabric slightly. Tack and sew.

Open the zip and place the two fabric circles right sides facing. Tack together round remaining circumference. Sew. Remove tacking. Notch the seam allowance. Turn to right side and insert pad.

Back zip opening

A back zip is easier to sew into a round cushion and looks neater because the zip is sewn between two pieces of flat fabric. Using the circular paper pattern, as before, cut just one piece of fabric (for the front of the cover). Choose a zip length about 10cm/4in shorter than the diameter and using the same circular paper pattern.

1 Mark a straight line across the paper pattern where the zip is to be fitted (you can place this centred or off centre) and cut the paper pattern across this line.

2 Position the two paper patterns on the fabric and mark an extra 1.5cm/⅝in seam allowance along both straight cut edges. Cut out with the extra seam allowance. Right sides facing, match the two straight edges and tack together. Sew 5cm/2in from either end along the seam allowance. Remove tacking. Sew in zip (as for square cushion cover). Open the zip. Right sides of the front and back circles facing, tack together and sew all round taking 1.5cm/⅝in seams. Remove the tacking. Turn the cover through to right side and add cushion pad.

11

Single frill with bias edge

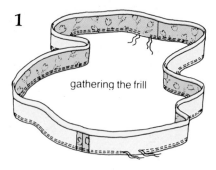

gathering the frill

1

This cushion cover has a frill made from a single thickness of fabric, the outer raw edge of which is finished with bias binding.

Cutting out and making up

Cut out two squares or rectangles of fabric to the cushion pad size with a 1.5cm/⅝in seam allowance all round. The finished width of the frill is a matter of personal choice, but you will find that a frill any wider than 7cm/2¾in finished width is rather floppy. Add 1.5cm/⅝in to finished width of frill for seam allowance. To calculate the length of frill required, measure all round the cushion cover and double this

Add contrast bias for impact.

figure to give an ample frill. For a thick fabric which is more bulky to gather, one-and-a-half times the length is sufficient.

For very fine fabrics only you may need two to three times the measurement.

To the frill length measurement add 3cm/1¼in seam allowance for joining the two short ends and add 3cm/1¼in for any joins that are necessary to make up the length. Cut out the frill and, with 1.5cm/⅝in seams, join the lengths to make a circle.

Neaten the outer raw edge of the

frill with bias binding.

1 Sew two lines of gathering stitches on the inner edge of the frill, 1.5cm/⅝in and 1cm/½in from raw edge. Work gathering stitches along half the length, then cut the stitching threads. Make gathering stitches along the remaining length in the same way.

With right side of frill facing right side of one of the main cushion cover pieces, and raw edges matching, gently ease up the gathering threads along half the frill length, until this exactly fits two sides of the cover fabric. Make slightly more gathers on the corners to allow sufficient fullness.

Pleated frill

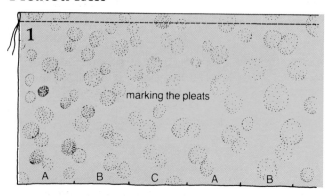

marking the pleats

1

A B C A B

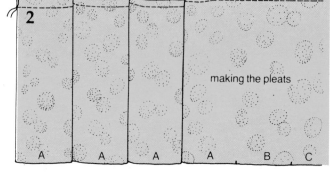

making the pleats

2

A A A A B C

A pleated fabric frill gives a crisp finish to a round or rectangular cushion cover. Piping can also be inserted into the seam for extra decorative effect.

Cutting out and making up

Cut out two squares or rectangles of fabric to the cushion pad size, with a 1.5cm/⅝in seam allowance all round. To calculate the amount of fabric length needed for the frill, measure all round cushion pad and cut fabric to three times this length plus 3cm/1¼in seam allowance for joining the two short ends and add 3cm/1¼in seam allowance for any

joins that are necessary to make up the complete frill length.

To calculate the amount of fabric width needed for the frill, decide on the finished width and add 2.5cm/1in for seams.

Cut out the frill fabric and join the pieces to make one length. On the outer long edge turn a 1cm/½in double hem (5mm/¼in and then 5mm/¼in) to the wrong side and sew.

To pleat up the frill mark the fabric into 3cm/1¼in sections along its length with tailor's chalk. Mark on the right side of the fabric, within the 1.5cm/⅝in seam allowance.

1 Starting at one edge, and using

tailor's chalk, lightly mark each section in a series of consecutive As, Bs and Cs along the length.

2 Make the pleats by folding and pressing the fabric on the right side on the chalk marks so that the mark between A and B is pressed and touches the mark between C and the next A. Continue along the length. From the right side, all the As should be visible and the Bs and Cs folded to the inside. Pin the pleats and tack. Machine 1cm/½in from raw edge. Remove tacking. Tack the pleated frill in place, as for the single frill with bias edge. (To add piping to the seam see under

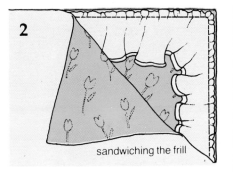

2

sandwiching the frill

Match and fit the remaining half of frill to the other two sides of the fabric in the same way. Tack the frill in place. Machine 1cm/½in from raw edge. Remove tacking and gathering threads.
At this stage add a side zip, if you want a zip opening.
2 With right sides together, place the second piece of cover fabric on the first, sandwiching the frill inside, and tack all round. Sew all round, allowing a 1.5cm/⅝in seam, and leaving an opening to insert the pad, if a zip has not been added. Remove tacking, turn through to the right side and insert the pad.

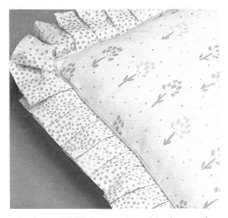

A pleated frill is smart and looks good on round and square cushions.

Professional Touch, right.)
If you want to add a side zip, do so at this stage.
Right sides facing, place the second cushion piece over the first, sandwiching the frill. Sew all round with a 1.5cm/⅝in seam and leave a gap for inserting the cushion pad if a zip has not been added. Remove all tacking. If you have added piping, use a zipper foot to get close up to the piping with the stitching line. Turn through to right side and insert the pad.

Covering piping cord

You can buy piping cord from haberdashery departments. It comes in several thicknesses, and your choice will depend on how prominent you want it to be – the thicker the cord, the more it will stand out from the seam. Piping cord has to be covered with fabric cut on the bias. Either you can make your own bias

strips from spare fabric or buy ready-made bias binding. In either case, you will need enough bias fabric to go right round the piping cord and to allow at least 1cm/½in on each edge for seam allowance. So for piping cord that is 12mm/½in in diameter, you will need bias strips at least 3.2cm/1⅜in wide.

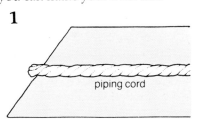

1

piping cord

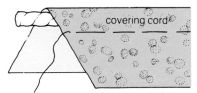

2

covering cord

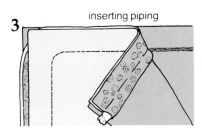

3

inserting piping

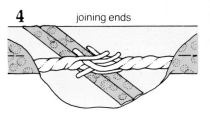

4

joining ends

1 Press the bias strip flat and place the piping cord along the centre, on the wrong side of the fabric.
2 Wrap the fabric round the piping cord and tack the fabric together as close to the cord as possible. Sew, using a zipper foot to get the stitching line close to the cord. Remove tacking.

Adding piping to a seam

Mark seam allowance (1.5cm/⅝in) on the right side of either the front or back of the cushion. cover, using tailor's chalk.
3 Place the piping on the right side of the cover, matching the stitching line of the piping to the marked seam allowance line. The raw edges of the bias piping cord fabric must face outwards to the raw edges of the cushion cover. Tack the piping in place. At each corner, curve the piping round slightly to avoid a sharp angle.
To join the piping first make a

Added to a seam, piping gives a professional and expensive look.

join in the bias strip along the grain. Join the piping cord by allowing an extra 5cm/2in when you cut the cord to length.
4 Overlap the two ends by 2.5cm/1in and at each end unravel the twisted cords and trim each separate cord to a slightly different length. Intertwine the cords at each end to make a smooth join.
Place front and back of cushion cover together. Tack together, except for the opening and taking a 1.5cm/⅝in seam, stitch as close to the piping cord as possible using the zipper foot on your machine. Sew the piping cord in place along the open edge. Remove tacking.

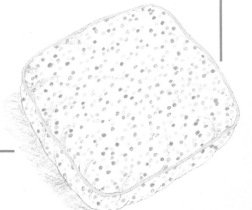

Zigzagged pointed frill

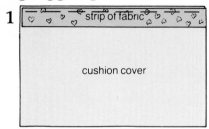

1 strip of fabric / cushion cover

2 fold

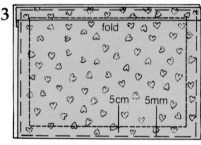

3 fold / 5cm / 5mm

This fancy edge is cut to shape with the help of a template and the raw edges neatly finished with a machine zigzag stitch. This type of cover is not suitable for a zip.

Cutting out and making up

Cut out two squares or rectangles of fabric to the cushion pad size plus an extra 8cm/3¼in on both the length and width. Also cut one strip of fabric 8cm/3¼in by the length of the rectangle or square.
1 Place 8cm/3¼in wide fabric strip wrong sides facing on one cushion cover rectangle/square, and with raw edges matching to one of the edges (a long edge if making a rectangular cover). Tack in place.

Take the other rectangle/square and turn 5cm/2in to the wrong side along one edge (long edge if a rectangle). Trim the turn to 3cm/1¼in.
2 Lay the two rectangles/squares together, wrong sides facing, matching raw edges and placing the folded edge of one rectangle/square so that it overlaps the attached strip on the other rectangle/square.
3 Tack all round cover, 5mm/¼in, then 5cm/2in from the raw edges.

Machine along the 5cm/2in tacking line, working from the back, so that the opening is not machined closed. Turn to right side.
To make the pointed frill You will need a cardboard template to cut an evenly pointed edge between the 5cm/2in machined line and the edges of the cushion cover. To make the template, cut a piece of card 30cm × 4.5cm/11¾in × 1¾in. Draw a central line through the length. Mark along

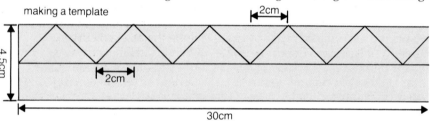

making a template
4.5cm
2cm
2cm
30cm

Double gathered frill

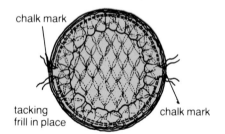

chalk mark
tacking frill in place
chalk mark

This frill is made from a double thickness of fabric. If you are using a fabric with a one-way design, you can create an interesting visual effect by cutting the frill fabric so that the design runs in the opposite direction to that on the cover.

Cutting out and making up

Cut out two circles of fabric to the cushion pad size with a 1.5cm/⅝in seam allowance all round. If you want to insert a back zip, do so at this stage.
To calculate the length of frill needed measure the circumference of your cushion pad with a tape measure. For full gathers cut the frill to double this measurement, adding 3cm/1¼in seam allowance for joining the two short ends and

This frill can be made in either a matching or a contrast fabric.

another 3cm/1¼in for each join necessary to make up the length. Decide on the finished width of the frill, double this measurement and add 3cm/1¼in seam allowance. Join the fabric strips to make up the total length, with 1.5cm/⅝in seams. Join the two short ends.
Fold the frill fabric in half lengthways, wrong sides facing and press. Work two rows of gathering stitches through the layers, 1.5cm/⅝in and 1cm/½in from the raw edges. Work the gathering along half the length, then cut the threads. Resume the gathering along the remaining length.
Fold one of the cushion cover circles

in half, and mark the raw edge at each end of the fold with a tailor's chalk line. Open flat again.
With raw edges matching, and frill length to right side of marked cover piece, place each break in the gathering threads on one of the chalk marks. Gently pull up the gathering threads, evenly around the circumference.
Tack frill in place. If you want to insert a side zip, do so at this stage.
Right sides facing, lay the remaining circle of fabric on the first, sandwiching the frill. Tack together and then machine with a 1.5cm/⅝in seam, and leave a gap to insert the pad if a zip has not been added. Remove tacking.
Turn through to right side and insert the pad.

Zigzag points make an unusual edging.

this line every 2cm/¾in and along outer edge of card every 2cm/¾in.
4 Join up the marks with diagonal lines to make a series of points. Cut along the diagonal lines. Lay the template with the straight edge along a section of the stitching and with tailor's chalk mark around the points on to the fabric. Continue in this way all around the cushion cover. At each corner, turn the template at an angle of 45°.
Using a small size, close machine zigzag, stitch along the marked points.
Using small sharp scissors, carefully cut away the fabric close to the zigzag stitching, so that you have a pointed frill. Insert pad.

Gathered corners with piping

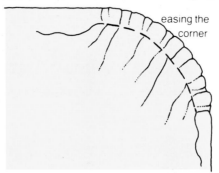

easing the corner

Gathered corners create a plump cushion.

This style of cover, suitable for a rectangular or square cushion, has slightly gathered corners.

Cutting out and making up
Cut out two squares or rectangles of fabric to the cushion pad size, with a 1.5cm/⅝in seam allowance all round. Curve each corner by drawing round a saucer or a glass with tailor's chalk. Cut the fabric along the chalked curves.
On both cushion cover pieces work a gathering thread round each corner and gently ease up gathering threads so that each corner is reduced by 3-4cm/1¼-1½in.

Cover the piping cord and stitch to the right side of one cushion cover piece (see Professional Touch on page 13), following the curves on the corners.
If you want to add a side zip, do so at this stage.
Lay both cushion pieces right sides facing and tack together. Sew all round with a zipper foot as close to the ridge of the piping as possible leaving a gap to insert the cushion pad if you have not added a zip.
Turn through to right side and insert pad.

Overlap frill with trimmed edge

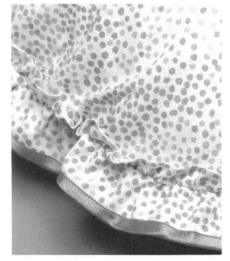

This frill looks best on a round cushion but can be used on a square too.

This is a double fabric frill with the folded edge gathered on to the top edge of the cushion cover. The two raw edges are joined together with satin bias binding.

Cutting out and making up
Cut out two circles of fabric to the pad size with a 1.5cm/⅝in seam

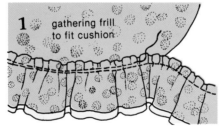

1 gathering frill to fit cushion

allowance all round.
If you want to insert a back zip, do so at this stage.
Calculate the length and width of frill needed as for the double gathered frill, but do not add a seam allowance to the finished width, as the raw edges are bias bound.
Cut the frill in fabric, join and press in half as for the double gathered frill. Tack the two raw edges together and neaten the raw edges by enclosing them in toning or contrasting bias binding.
Work gathering stitches in two halves along the folded edge as for the double gathered frill.
1 Gather up the frill to fit the circumference of the cushion, placing folded edge of gathered frill 4cm/1½in in from the raw

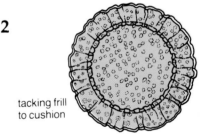

2

tacking frill to cushion

edge of the right side of fabric circle, so that the frill overlaps the circle by 4cm/1½in all round. Tack in place.
2 Top stitch frill to the circle of fabric, 2cm/¾in from the folded edge. Remove tacking and gathering threads.
Fold the frill to the centre of the fabric circle.
Insert a zip at this stage, if you are adding a side zip.
Place the remaining circle on first circle, right sides facing, and tack together all round through both layers of fabric – make sure the frill does not get caught in the stitching. Sew with a 1.5cm/⅝in seam and leave a gap to insert the cushion pad if a zip has not been added.
Turn through to right side and insert pad.

Gusseted cushions for a perfect fit

Make feather filled cushions luxuriously deep and foam filled cushions neatly tailored, by adding a third dimension – a side gusset – to the cover. Even the plainest of kitchen chairs can be transformed with a bright, comfortable cushion.

Adding a gusset to a cushion cover allows for a deeper, more tailored shape. The gusset, or welt, as it is sometimes known, is a strip of fabric forming the sides between the top and bottom pieces of the cover. The three-dimensional shape produced can be emphasized by piped seams or a decorative or contrasting gusset.

A zip inserted in one side makes it easier to remove the cover for cleaning. If you do not want a zipped opening (or for an inner cover), omit the instructions for a zip. Leave one side unstitched, except for 5cm/2in at the corners, then slipstitch together after inserting cushion pad or stuffing. For soft fillings such as feather, down or foam chips, simply add the zip to one side of the cover and squash the cushion through the opening. For solid fillings such as foam pads, you may have to extend the zip around the adjoining sides – in which case, take this into account when measuring up for the cushion cover fabric.

Before you begin making up these cushions, read the previous chapter for basic instructions.

Right: This antique wooden bench is made more comfortable with a firm, gusseted seat cushion in an attractive print. The round, feather-filled cushions are made in plain, toning fabrics.

Making square and rectangular cushions

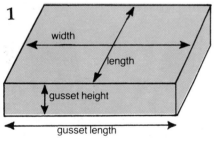

1 For the top and bottom piece of the cushion cover measure the surface of the pad in both directions and add an extra 1.5cm/⅝in seam allowance all round.

For gusset pieces, measure the width and height of each side of the pad and add 1.5cm/⅝in seam allowance all round. The back gusset piece will be cut in half along its length for the zip to be inserted, so add an extra 3cm/1¼in to the height of this piece.

For each cushion cover, cut out from fabric one top piece, one bottom piece and the four gusset pieces – one back, one front and two sides.

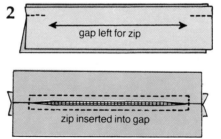

2 Cut the back gusset piece in half along its length and place the two halves right sides together. Rejoin the cut edge by tacking for approximately 5cm/2in from each corner along the seamline, leaving a central opening to fit the zip. Stitch, press the seam flat and insert the zip.

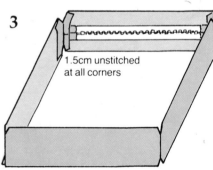

3 With right sides facing, and taking a 1.5cm/⅝in seam allowance, join the four gusset pieces together to form a square or rectangle. Leave 1.5cm/⅝in at each end of seams unstitched but secure ends of stitching firmly. Press seams open.

4 Matching seams to corners and with right sides facing, pin and tack gusset to one main piece. Machine in place with a 1.5cm/⅝in seam. To ensure a neat square finish at the corners, insert the machine needle right into the fabric at the corner, lift the presser foot, then turn the fabric to correct position for the next row of machining, pivoting it around

Making round cushions

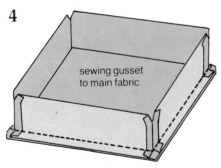

sewing gusset to main fabric

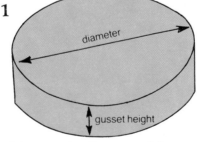

diameter

gusset height

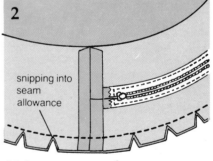

snipping into seam allowance

the needle. Replace presser foot and continue stitching.

Snip diagonally across seam allowance at corners, close to stitching, to eliminate bulk. Open the zip, then attach remaining main piece in the same way. Press all seams towards gusset. Turn cover through to right side and insert cushion pad.

1 Measure the diameter of the cushion pad and add 3cm/1¼in to give the diameter of the circles to cut for the top and bottom of the cushion cover.

Measure the circumference and the height of the pad. Cut one gusset piece as a rectangle measuring half the circumference plus 3cm/1¼in by the height plus 3cm/1¼in.

Cut a second rectangle for the zipped half of the gusset but adding a further 3cm/1¼in to the height. Cut this piece in half along its length, place the two halves right sides together, rejoin at each end and insert zip as for square cushion.

Make up gusset as for square one, but forming a circle.

2 With the zip open and right sides together, attach top and bottom circles to the gusset, snipping into the seam allowance all the way round to ease the fabric and give a neat appearance to the seam on the right side. Press all seams towards gusset. Turn cover through to right side and insert pad.

A bolster cushion is simply a variation of a round gusseted cushion, with the gusset height extended to the required length of bolster. Cut the gusset in one piece and insert the zip in the seam.

17

Making shaped cushions

Many chairs have arms or staves that jut out into the seat, so the cushions must fit an irregular shape. If you already have cushion pads to fit the chair, cut the pattern pieces to fit these – adding 1.5cm/⅝in seam allowance all round. If not, make a paper pattern of the seat shape.

1 Measure the width and depth of the chair seat and cut a piece of paper a little larger. Lay the paper on the seat and fold in the edges to the exact outline of the seat. Cut out this shape and check its accuracy by laying it on the seat once more; adjust if necessary. If a back cushion is needed for a sofa or armchair make a paper pattern in the same way, remembering that it will sit on top of the seat cushion, so measure up from the height of this. You can now use these patterns to have pieces of foam cut for the pads. Depending on the amount of padding required, the usual depth for seat pads is 5-10cm/2-4in. Alternatively, you could use your pattern to make up an inner cover in ticking or down-proof cambric, omitting the zip. Stuff with feathers, feather and down or foam chips and sew up opening. Feather cushions look soft and luxurious

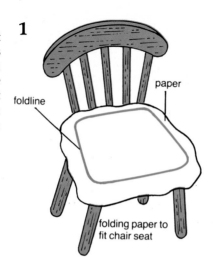

foldline · paper

folding paper to fit chair seat

but a foam pad retains its shape better and looks neater.

2 After measuring up the shaped pad, calculate the length and position of the zip. On a wedge-shaped cushion, the zip can be inserted into the gusset but it should extend at least 5cm/2in around each adjoining side, so the back gusset piece must be lengthened and the sides correspondingly shortened.

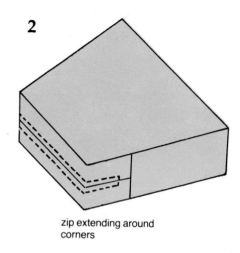

zip extending around corners

3 For cushions with curved sections cut out to accommodate the arms of the chair, insert the zip into the widest part of the bottom piece of the cushion cover, where it will not show. Cut across your paper pattern where the zip is to go and add 1.5cm/⅝in seam allowance to each edge, before cutting from fabric. The gusset will then consist of side pieces simply joined at the corners, or wherever is most inconspicuous, depending on the irregularity of the shape.

Cut out and make up as for square cushions, placing zip in gusset or main bottom piece as necessary.

Attaching the cushion to the chair

Although the cushions simply lie in place on sofas and easy chairs, when used on wooden upright chairs, stools and rocking chairs they need to be firmly attached. Ties are the simplest solution. They can be made from coloured ribbons or cord, purchased bias binding or tape, or bias strips cut from spare fabric. (Fold raw edges of bias strip to centre, fold strip in half lengthways to enclose them, tuck in short raw ends and slipstitch together). For each tie you need about a 30cm/12in length.

Ties for chairs Place the ties as near to the back corner of the cushion pad as possible, matching up their position to the struts of the chair. Securely stitch centre of tie to cover, then simply tie round chair strut.

Ties for stools Add a tie to each lower corner of the cushion and tie behind stool legs or, for a decorative finish, cross ties behind the legs and tie a bow in front.

Velcro fastenings Use Velcro as an

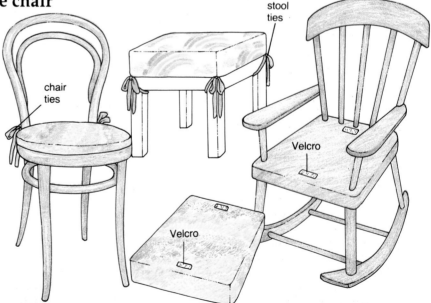

stool ties · chair ties · Velcro · Velcro

alternative to a tie for an invisible fixing – two 5cm/2in lengths are sufficient for one cushion. Stitch one half of each Velcro piece to centre front and centre back of the cushion's underside about 3cm/1¼in

in from the edge. Using a clear household adhesive, stick the backs of remaining Velcro pieces to chair seat to correspond. Allow glue to dry completely before putting cushion in place.

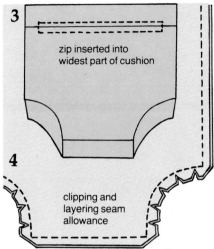

3

zip inserted into widest part of cushion

4

clipping and layering seam allowance

4 To give a perfect finish to the cushion cover, once the stitching is complete, trim away some of the seam allowance to layer the seams and reduce fabric bulk. Snip into the seam allowance on curves, cutting away small V shapes on inner curves, clipping right up to – but not through – stitching line. At the corners, snip off the seam allowance diagonally.
Press all seams towards the gusset. Turn through to right side – all the seams should now lie perfectly flat.

Right: Soften the seat of a rocking chair with a pretty piped cushion.

Finishing touches

To make cushions really special – and individual – add one of the following finishes:
Piped edges These give an elegant tailored finish. Use them to pick out one of the colours on a patterned fabric, or pipe in a toning or contrasting colour to add emphasis to a plain cover. Make up the piping and tack it in position round the edges of both main pieces. Make up covers, sewing the gussets in place using a zipper or piping foot and stitching as close to the piping as possible.
Mix and match fabrics Many fabric ranges now include co-ordinated patterned or plain fabrics, matching borders and positive/negative designs. Use an alternative to the main fabric for the gusset, and perhaps also use the alternative fabric for scatter cushions.
Pleated gussets Join gusset strips to make three times the required length plus seam allowances. Pleat up, tack and then stitch along just inside seamline to hold pleats firmly in position before inserting gusset.

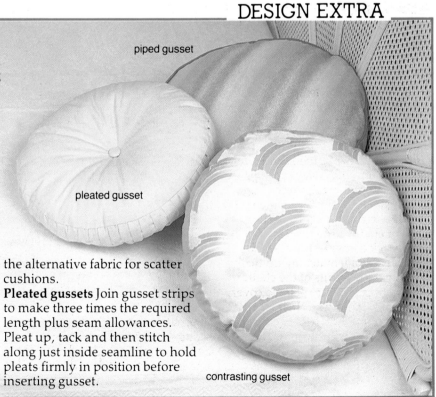

piped gusset

pleated gusset

contrasting gusset

Soft seating:
sag bags and floor cushions

*If you're short of space – or of money – for extra seating,
then floor cushions or sag bags provide
the answer. They make comfortable, inexpensive seating units
that can easily be tucked out of the way,
and firm foam cushions will even double as a mattress.*

Use floor cushions or sag bags to replace traditional settees and armchairs for a relaxed informal look that is inexpensive to create and easily varied. They are also ideal as extra seating that can be brought out for visitors then pushed into the background, or into a cupboard, when not required.

Choose a firm furnishing fabric or a tough fabric such as corduroy for the covers. A reasonably dark shade is more practical but all the covers are zipped and easily removed for cleaning.

Sag bags have always been popular with children and teenagers but they are surprisingly comfortable for adults too. Sink into a sag bag and the polystyrene bead filling moulds itself to support your favourite sitting position. This sag bag has a handy

Above: Sag bags are great fun and surprisingly comfortable. For maximum safety, use a fire-retardant polystyrene granule filling.

strap at the top which makes it easy to move around – try one in the garden on a sunny day.

Fabric-covered foam blocks make particularly versatile floor cushions – stack three together against the wall as a simple chair, tie them in line to form a single mattress, use more for a settee, or simply sit on one!

A foam specialist shop will cut the foam to the exact size you require. It is advisable to make a cotton inner cover to protect the foam and help to prevent the corners and edges crumbling with age. This inner cover does not need a zip as it will not need to be removed for cleaning.

Before making up your floor cushion, read pages 16-17 for detailed instructions for cutting out and making up a gusseted cover.

Making a sag bag

Make the sag bag by sewing together six identical pattern pieces, rather like the segments of an orange, and adding a circular zipped base.

Fill the bag with polystyrene granules or beads to about two-thirds of its capacity – the surplus space means you can push the bag into the most comfortable shape for sitting on.

You will need

3.40m/3¾yd of fabric 120cm/48in wide
46cm/18in zip
Matching thread
2.70kg/6lb bag of polystyrene granules

Preparing the pattern pieces

Enlarge the segment pattern piece given below by drawing a grid on which one square equals 5cm/2in and copying the outline on to it square by square. (A 1.5cm/⅝in seam allowance is included.)

Using this as the paper pattern, cut six segment shapes from your fabric. On the wrong side of each segment, draw a chalk line about 5cm/2in down from the pointed end (see graph below).

Cut two strips of fabric each 35cm × 6cm/14in × 2¾in for the handle. Cut a circle 64cm/25in in diameter for the base. Fold the circle across the diameter and cut in half.

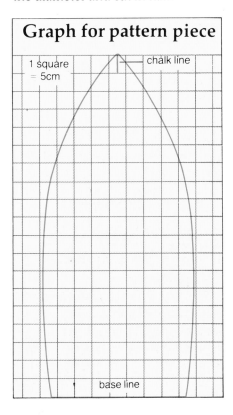

Graph for pattern piece

1 square = 5cm

chalk line

base line

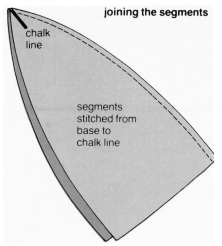

joining the segments

chalk line

segments stitched from base to chalk line

Making up

Joining the segments Place two segments right sides together. On one side only, tack and then stitch from the base up to the point where the seamline meets the chalk line. In the same way attach a third segment to the free side of one of the first two, stitching as far as the chalk line.

Repeat this procedure to join the remaining three segments together as a separate half.

Adding the handle Make up the handle by placing the two strips right sides together and sewing down both long edges. Turn right side out, press and tack the ends to the outside edges of one set of three segments 2cm/1in below the top point, raw edges together.

Place the two sets of three segments together, right sides facing, sandwiching the handle ends, and tack and stitch the two remaining outer edges from base to chalk line. Turn right side out and the handle will protrude from the seams. Reinforce the point at which the segments meet with a little hand stitching – this gives added strength to the area most under stress.

Press the seams open, then run a double row of gathering stitches around the base, just within the seam allowance.

Making the base Place the two halves of the circle right sides together and stitch along the straight edge for 9cm/3½in from each end. Press the seam allowances open and insert the zip in the central gap.

With the zip open, and right sides facing, pin the base of three segments around half of the circle,

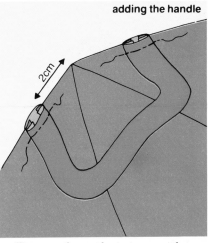

adding the handle

2cm

pulling up the gathers to ease the fitting. Pin the other three segments to the remaining half of the circle; gather, tack and stitch all round. Turn right side out through the open zip.

Filling the sag bag

Fill about two-thirds of the bag with polystyrene granules.

As a precaution against the bag being opened accidentally or by an inquisitive child, hand stitch the pulling tab of the zip to the base of the bag.

Save any left-over granules as they do tend to crush down a bit with time and wear, and the sag bag may need topping up.

Laundering the cover

To empty the bag for laundering, shake the granules to the bottom of the sag bag, hold over a large open plastic sack and open the zip. Gently shake the granules from the sag bag into the plastic sack – it is easier if you have a helper so that one person can hold the plastic sack while the other tips up.

Turn the sag bag cover inside out, pick out any remaining granules caught in the seams or stuck to the inside of the fabric and wash or dry clean according to the type of fabric.

If your sag bag is likely to be washed frequently, it is worth making an inner cover which can be removed complete with the polystyrene granules while the outer cover is being laundered. Make the inner cover from an inexpensive fabric such as calico, following the sag bag pattern but omitting the handle and zip.

21

Making foam block cushions

Cover a block of foam with a simple gusseted cover and you have a comfortable floor cushion. Make more than one cushion, inserting ties into the seams, and the potential variations of seating are endless.

The instructions are for a versatile 75cm/30in square cushion, 18cm/7in deep, but alter the measurements to suit your needs, remembering to adjust the fabric requirements accordingly.

You will need

75cm/30in square block of dense, seating quality foam approximately 18cm/7in deep
2.5m/2¾yd of fabric at least 80cm/32in wide for the top cover
The same amount of a firm plain fabric such as pre-shrunk calico for the inner cover, if required
70cm/28in zip
Thread
Strong cotton tape about 15mm/⅝in wide to make the ties

Cutting out

For the top cover cut two pieces of fabric 78cm/31¼in square, three gusset strips each 78cm/31¼in wide and 21cm/8¼in deep, and one strip for the back gusset piece the same width but 24cm/9½in deep.
Cut the inner cover pieces to the same dimensions but make all four gusset strips 21cm/8¼in deep. These dimensions include 1.5cm/⅝in seam allowances.

Making up

Make up the inner cover in the same way as a gusseted cushion cover, insert the foam block and hand stitch the opening together. Make the top cover in the same way as a gusseted cushion cover but cutting the back gusset piece in half, widthways, and inserting the zip between.

Adding ties If you wish to link cushions together, insert ties in the seams while making up.

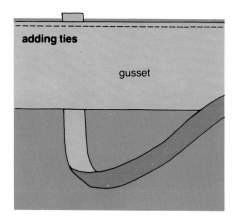

adding ties

gusset

Cut a 30cm/12in length of cotton tape for each tie required. (If you cannot buy the colour of tape to match or contrast with your cushion, dye white tape with a commercial fabric dye.) Eight lengths of tape – two on two opposite sides on both top and bottom – give complete versatility.

Below: Vary the shape and size of cushion to suit your needs – a half-size cushion makes a good back-rest.

Soft floor cushions

These giant floor cushions are quick and easy to make using ready-made cushion pads filled with foam chips or feathers. Simply measure the pad and make up a basic cover as described on pages 8-10, inserting a zip in the side seam for easy removal for cleaning. A combination of large and small floor cushions can make versatile, cheap seating. Use them to replace conventional chairs – an arrangement of low level tables and cushions as shown here gives a feeling of space to a small area and is inexpensive to create. Choose one dominant colour or a combination of toning colours for the best effect. These cushions are made up in a series of black and white checked fabrics, the checks decreasing with the size of the cushions, to give a co-ordinated yet varied look. Alternatively, one or two large

Above: Floor cushions replace the conventional three-piece suite to provide interesting and versatile seating at a fraction of the cost.

cushions are a useful addition to sofa and chairs and a pile of bright covers can add a splash of colour to a dull corner. Bear in mind when choosing fabrics that floor cushions will get a greater amount of wear than a sofa cushion so use a tough furnishing fabric.

23

Simple unlined curtains – the lightweight look

Unlined curtains involve a minimum of sewing and are the simplest type to make up. Join fabric widths, neaten side hems, add heading tape, sew bottom hems and you're there. Sheer fabrics – the kind that let in lots of light and give you privacy too – are highly suitable for making up by this quick method.

Unlined curtains are ideal for use in kitchens, bathrooms, playrooms or on any window where insulation and light exclusion are less important than a cheap and cheerful effect and easy laundering. Unlined curtains are also the simplest to make.

Double hems neaten edges and standard curtain tape attached to the top has pockets for the hooks which hang the curtain on the track. For curtains that do not need to be drawn back, a cased heading hung on elasticated wire or a length of dowelling is an even cheaper alternative.

Choosing and buying fabrics

All furnishing fabric departments include a wide range of plain and printed cottons ideal for unlined curtains. Many dressmaking fabrics are also suitable, although they may tend to fade more quickly.

There is also a wide choice of semi-transparent fabrics, usually in man-made fibres and often incorporating a woven thread pattern. Curtains made from these sheer fabrics usually remain drawn to provide privacy while letting in light and are also excellent for disguising a far from scenic view.

Instructions for measuring up for curtains are given on page 26 but bear in mind that some washable fabrics have a tendency to shrink: if in doubt buy an extra 10% of fabric length (10cm/4in for every metre/yard). Either wash the fabric before cutting out or make up with all the excess incorporated in the bottom hem. The curtain can then be let down after the first wash.

The sewing thread should match the fibre content of the fabric. A polyester thread is best for man-made fabrics. Sheers, man-made fabrics in particular, tend to slip when machining so tacking is essential. Fine pins and machine needles should be used and the tension set fairly loose. Use a scrap of spare fabric to test stitch size and tension before beginning. Fabrics which are very slippery or have an open weave can be machined by placing tissue paper between the machine base plate and fabric – to be torn away later.

Joining widths Curtain fabrics come in fairly standard widths. Try to buy the widest possible to avoid seams, but if necessary, join widths with a flat or French seam. See page 44 for matching patterns.

Selvedges, if they are woven more tightly than the rest of the fabric, should be trimmed off before seaming to prevent puckering. If selvedges are left, they should be clipped every 10cm/4in along the edge.

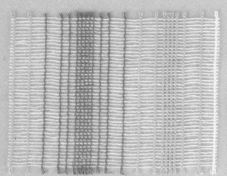

Above: In this bay window corner, full length sheer curtains soften the effect of plain roller blinds.
Left: The variety of fibres and weaving/ printing techniques makes for an abundant choice of sheer fabrics, from fine nets to heavier lace designs and open weaves.

25

Measuring up

The curtain track or pole can be either in the window recess (most net curtains are hung in this position) or outside the recess and just above the window frame.

If the track is *outside* the recess, it should extend, if possible, 15cm/6in on each side of the window frame so that the curtains can be pulled back from the glass area during the day for maximum light. The height of the track above the window will depend on the best visual effect for the curtain length you choose. Lightweight sheer fabrics hung *inside* a window recess can be supported by a thin pole or elasticated wire slotted through a casing at the top of the curtain. A pole can also look good outside the recess.

How much fabric do you need? This method of calculating the total amount of fabric needed should be used for all curtains, lined or unlined. You may find that a pocket calculator is helpful.

1 Measure the total width needed
2 Work out number of fabric widths required
3 Multiply fabric widths by length to arrive at a total amount.

For a six-step guide to calculating your fabric needs see far right.

Width Measure the width of your track or pole using a steel tape or wooden rule. Multiply this figure by 1½ to 3 times depending on the heading tape. Standard heading tape, such as Rufflette 'Standard', needs at least 1½ – 2 times the track width in fabric. Light sheers can use up to three times. To the total width required, add on 2.5cm/1in for each side hem on the curtains (5cm/2in for sheers) and add the overlap for each curtain if the track is in two overlapping halves. Divide this total figure by the fabric width chosen for number of fabric widths needed. Err on the generous side, rounding up to full widths as you will need 3cm/1¼in seam allowance for each width join.

Length Measure the curtain length (see diagrams below). Add 4cm/1½in for top heading hem (Standard heading tape) and 15cm/6in for bottom hem. For sheer fabrics double this bottom hem allowance and add 6cm/2¼in for top hem for cased heading.

Pattern repeats If your fabric has a definite pattern, you must make an allowance for matching. As a guideline, add one extra pattern repeat for every fabric width. Pattern matching is covered in detail on page 44.

Six-step guide to fabric calculation

Taking curtain track width and finished curtain length, follow this step-by-step method to arrive at the total quantity of fabric required.

1 Measure width of track
2 Multiply track width by 1½-2 (for Standard heading tape) or by up to 3 times for other heading tapes and add side hem allowances (double for sheers). Add overlap fabric allowance if applicable.
3 Divide this figure by the width of fabric to give number of fabric widths.
4 This will probably not work out to a whole number of widths, so round this figure up to the next full width.
5 Multiply the number of fabric widths by length of curtain with top hem and bottom hem allowances to give total fabric needed.
6 This total has now to be divided between the number of curtains (generally two).

sill length

just below sill length

floor length

How long should your curtains be?

This is a matter of personal choice, and depends on the size of the window, your style of furnishings and the visual effect you want but basically curtain lengths fall into three categories: sill length, just below sill length (15–20cm/6–8in) and floor length.

Making up the curtains

Preparing to cut

You need a large flat surface that will take the complete length of your curtain and a full width of the fabric. A large table is best, or clear an area of floor space to work on. If you work in cramped conditions, you're likely to make mistakes in measuring and cutting out. You'll need space for an ironing board too.

Cutting out

It's vitally important that you start with a straight cut across the width. If the fabric has a straight thread pattern (the weft) across the width, pull out a thread for a straight line, otherwise cut at a right angle to the selvedges. Line up the pattern repeat (if necessary) before cutting subsequent widths.

Joining widths

Seam widths of fabric together to make up the total width for each curtain. If the curtain contains full widths and a half, place the half width on the outer side of the curtain. Use a flat seam if the edges are selvedges or for raw edges that can be neatly finished off. To hide raw edges use fell or French seams.

Seams for joining widths

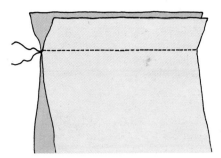 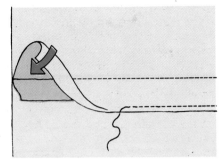 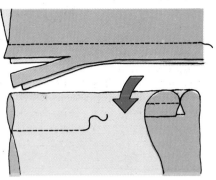

Flat seam
Right sides of fabric facing and edges matching, pin the two layers of fabric together and tack. Stitch 1.5cm/⅝in from edges. Remove tacking, press seam open. If the fabric edges are selvedges, clip seam allowance every 10cm/4in along the selvedge to prevent fabric puckering.

Fell seam
Right sides facing, make a flat seam of 1.5cm/⅝in. Press open. Trim one seam allowance in half. Fold other seam allowance over trimmed one and tack down to enclose raw edge. Top stitch through all layers. Remove tacking and press. One stitching line will show on right side of fabric.

French seam
Wrong sides facing, make a flat seam of 5mm/¼in. Trim to 3mm/⅛in. Press. Turn so right sides face and seam is on the fold. Tack the two layers together. Sew 1cm/½in down from first seam. Remove tacking. All raw edges are enclosed in seam and are to the reverse of the fabric. No stitching line shows on the right side of fabric.

Side hems

To neaten sides, turn 5mm/¼in of the hem allowance to wrong side and press. Fold remaining 2cm/¾in of hem allowance to wrong side. Tack. Stitch through all layers by machine or slipstitch. Remove all tacking. Slipstitch by passing the sewing needle through 1cm/½in of hem fold, picking up a single thread of the main fabric and then passing through 1cm/½in of fold again. Repeat down hem. Remove tacking. Sheer fabrics should be finished with a double side hem to look neat and prevent raw edges from showing through. Fold the 2.5cm/1in hem allowance to the wrong side and press. Fold over again to same size. Tack through all layers. Machine stitch or slipstitch in place.

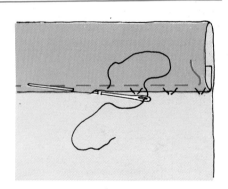

Hems for open weave fabrics

As with all sheer fabrics, side and bottom hems must be sewn with double turnings. You'll need to plan the placing of these hems so that the weave or pattern matches when the hem is turned under and also so that there's a maximum of solid pattern area available to sew through. In approximately the right position for the first turn of the hem, mark, with tailor's chalk or tacking, a vertical line between the pattern repeats (horizontal for bottom hems).
1 Mark again between the next line of pattern repeats.
2 Fold the fabric to the wrong side along the first marked line, and the pattern of the main fabric and turned under hem should match. Tack.

3 Turn the hem again along the second line. Tack and stitch. Remove tacking.
If the pattern is large, mark a suitable hem allowance and match pattern areas as best as possible. Use French seams to join widths taking care to match the pattern repeat as for hems.

Choosing the right heading tape

A heading tape is designed to take up the fullness of the curtain fabric in even gathers or pleats. Various styles of ready-made heading tapes are available, and the choice will depend on the gathered/pleated effect you personally find most pleasing. Standard tape gives an evenly gathered heading while deeper tapes are made to create various pleat effects – eg, Rufflette Regis produces very close deep pleats. Cartridge wider pleats and Tridis, fan-shaped triple pleats (see pages 38 and 39).

The synthetic fibre version of Standard tape is particularly suitable for sheers and lightweight fabrics. When you buy heading tape, check with the retailer how much fullness of fabric is required for the tape chosen. Rufflette Standard Tape for example requires a minimum of 1½ times track width, Regis 2½ times.

Attaching Standard heading tape

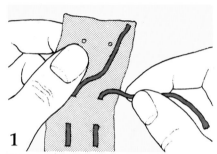

1

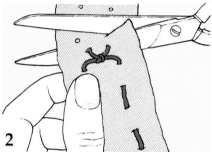

2

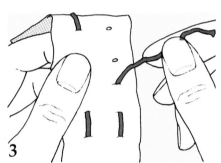

3

Measure finished width of curtain and add 4cm/1½in at either end for neatening. Cut a piece of heading tape to this length.
1 At the end where the curtains will overlap, pull 4cm/1½in of each cord free at the back of the tape.

On the wrong side of the heading tape, tie the 4cm/1½in of free cords together securely with a knot.
2 Trim off the surplus tape to leave 1.5cm/⅝in beyond the knot and press this seam allowance to the wrong side of the tape.

3 At the other end of the heading tape, gently ease out 4cm/1½in of cords on the right side. These cords will be used to pull the tape and fabric into gathers. Turn surplus tape to wrong side and press.

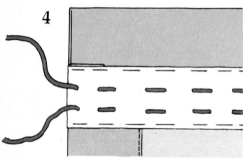

4

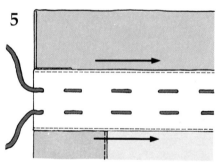

5

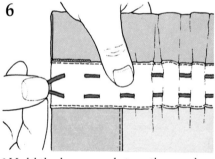

6

Turn 4cm/1½in at the head of the curtain to wrong side and press. Position the tape on the wrong side of curtain with top edge no more than 2.5cm/1in below the head.
4 Tack, tucking knot at centre side edge to wrong side.

5 Machine stitch the heading tape to curtain. Do not stitch across the short end with the loose cords. Stitch both long edges in the same direction as this will prevent any puckering while sewing. Remove tacking.

6 Hold the loose cords together and gently push tape up to gather the fabric until fully pleated.
Then ease out evenly until curtain is the right width.
Tie loose cords together. Insert tape hooks about every 8cm/3in.

Bottom hems

At bottom edge, turn 1cm/½in to wrong side and press. Turn balance of hem allowance to wrong side and pin. (For sheers see previous page.) Tack hem. Press complete curtain and hang on the track or pole for several days to allow fabric to 'drop'. Check level and height of hem and adjust if necessary. Slipstitch hem by hand and remove tacking. Sheer fabrics need a double hem, to hide raw edges, and look best with machined hems. Fold half the hem allowance to the wrong side and press. Fold the same amount again and tack hem (see diagram right). Hang for a few days. Check height and level and machine or slipstitch the hem. Remove tackings. Press.

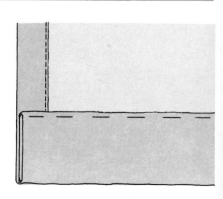

Choosing, making and caring for net curtains

Net curtains come in a wide range of plain, patterned and frilled sheer fabrics. Learn the most economical way of buying curtaining to suit the proportions of your window and keep unsightly joins to a minimum using these cutting and sewing techniques.

Net, lace and sheer curtains let in light while retaining privacy. They also filter harsh sunlight without totally obscuring the view, adding a fresh, decorative touch to the room scheme. Forget the old image of yellowing nets hanging limply from drooping wire – with recent developments in the design and manufacturing of sheer fabrics and hanging methods, there are now endless ways of styling them to create attractive window treatments.

Traditionally, net or lace curtains are hung permanently across the window recess, with heavier curtains on top. This gives scope for adding colourful trimmings, for using frilled or shaped curtaining, and for making use of modern curtain headings. Alternatively, try decorative lacy drapes over a simple roller blind, which is pulled down for warmth and privacy, or make a pretty sheer or net fabric into an Austrian blind, trimmed to echo the colours of top curtains.

Below: Modern net and sheer fabrics give you privacy with style.

Buying net curtain fabric

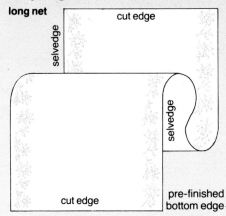

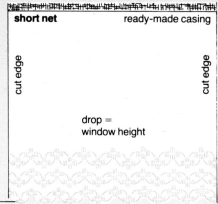

As seams in sheer curtains, particularly nets, tend to be very obvious against the light of a window, curtain net fabrics are sold in a wide variety of widths and drops to eliminate the need for seaming widths together.

Buying nets can be confusing – you can choose the fabric either in a suitable width (long nets) or with a suitable drop (short nets).

Long nets are sold in widths up to about 300cm/118in so that most curtains can be made from one piece of fabric, avoiding joins. The selvedges of the fabric form the side edges of the curtain. Measure the width of the window area to be covered and multiply this by 1½-3, according to the amount of fullness required, to calculate the width of curtain to buy.

Measure the height of the window area and add allowances for a top casing or turning, and a bottom hem, to calculate the length of curtaining to buy.

Short nets are ideal for windows that are wide rather than tall. They are manufactured so that the two edges of the fabric become the top and bottom of the curtain. One edge is pre-finished into a bottom hem, often with a frill, scallop or some other decorative finish, and the other edge has a casing to take either an elastic wire or a hanging rod. You therefore buy the *width* of fabric (called the drop) to fit the *height* of your window.

To determine the length of fabric to buy, multiply the width of the window area to be covered by 1½-3 times, according to how much fullness you require. The cut edges become the sides of the curtain and should be neatened with narrow double hems.

If you cannot buy the exact width that provides the drop of fabric that

Caring for and hanging net curtains

Some lace and sheer fabrics, particularly those in natural fibres such as cotton, can shrink by as much as 10% so buy sufficient fabric to allow for this if necessary. Wash and dry the fabric before cutting out so that any shrinkage has already occurred before making it up.

Check washing instructions when purchasing sheers as some of the more delicate fabrics can be damaged by machine washing. If in any doubt, wash gently by hand. If nylon nets turn yellow after a while try soaking them in a nylon whitener.

Net curtains are generally very light in weight so the method of hanging

does not have to be as bulky and strong as a standard type of curtain track. Nor do they need to be drawn back and forth as they are usually positioned permanently across the window.

Elasticated wire, with a small hook screwed in at each end, is the cheapest and most often used way to hang permanently positioned nets. This plastic-coated wire simply threads through the casing at the top of the curtain and, stretched taut, hooks to screw eyes inserted at either side of the window frame. It is suitable for small lightweight curtains but, unless put under very strong tension, tends to sag with large or

a selection of
sheer curtain fabrics

you need, buy the next size up and carefully unpick the top casing. Trim away any surplus fabric and remake the casing to the required depth so that the fabric is the exact drop required.

Stitching techniques for nets

Because of the transparency of nets, care must be taken in making hems and seams. Avoid seams where possible. If you have exceptionally large windows and cannot make a curtain from just one width of fabric, rather than joining fabric widths, make up two (or as many as necessary) separate curtains. Hang them next to each other and conceal the overlapping edges of the fabric in the folds of the curtain.

Hems should be double so that the raw edge of the fabric lies at the fold of the hem. If you have a deep hem on a patterned fabric and the pattern showing through the hem looks unsightly, insert a ribbon or a strip of fabric (the same width as the hem depth) into the hem so that only the solid colour shows through. The ribbon or fabric strip must have the same fibre content as the curtain, as should sewing thread and any heading tape used. See pages 27 and 33 for details of sewing hems and cased headings on sheer or net curtains.

Right: A length of lacy net transforms a bare window in a matter of minutes. Simply machine hem the ends and drape over a wooden pole and side brackets.

heavier curtains.

Curtain rods, designed for net or lightweight curtains that will not need to be drawn back and forth, also thread through the casing but – being in a rigid material – will not sag. Most of the rods designed for net curtains consist of two sections slotted together so that they are telescopic and easily adjustable to the exact size of the window. The rods simply sit on small hook-type fittings attached to the window frame. At least one manufacturer supplies the fittings backed with self-adhesive pads so they are easy to attach even to metal window frames.

Curtain track is required when net or lace curtains may need to be drawn back, perhaps to open French doors or to reveal large windows on a sunny day. Several tracks are specifically designed to be suitable for nets and lightweight curtains, and can be fixed to the wall or to the underside of a window recess. The curtains must have a taped – rather than a cased – heading so that hooks can be inserted to hang them on the track.

Heading for net curtains A cased heading is simple to make (see page 33) and gives a pretty gathered effect, but you may prefer to use a curtain heading tape for a more stylish finish. Some ordinary curtain tapes tend to be too heavy

for nets and even those that are lightweight must be used with proper curtain track. However, a translucent man-made fibre tape specifically designed for nets is now available. It draws the fabric into neat pencil pleats, but differs from other pencil pleating tapes in having bars on the back that simply thread on to an elasticated wire or narrow rod for hanging. Alternatively, the tape also has pockets which enable it to be hung with curtain hooks from a curtain track or decorative pole.

Attach the heading tape to the top of the curtain in the usual way, then pull up the two cords to form the pleating.

Cased headings

Not all curtains have to be hung from tracks. When positioning fixed curtains either inside a window recess or in front of the window, a quick and effective method is to use an elasticated wire, or a brass or wooden rod, slotted through a casing at the top of the curtain. This is particularly suitable for lightweight sheers which are not to be drawn back and forth, and are used to give permanent privacy at a window. When estimating fabric for this method, allow 12cm/5in for the heading (more if rod is thick).

Turn 6cm/2½in to wrong side on top of curtain and press. Fold over again 6cm/2½in. Tack. Sew along lower edge of hem and again 2.5cm/1in higher up. Remove tacking and press. This forms the casing. If the rod is thicker than 1cm/½in diameter, measure the diameter and add 1.5cm/⅝in to give a casing depth into which the rod will slip easily. Add 3.5cm/1¾in and double this total figure. Make up as above, but with a deeper casing. Insert rod or wire through the casing, easing the fabric into gathers.

The fabric between the top line of casing stitching and the curtain head forms a frill.

Left: These sheer curtains hang from a dowel rod slotted through a top casing. Below: A half curtain supported on elasticated wire through a narrow casing.
Opposite: Instructions for making a combined curtain/valance are given on page 34.

Creative ways to style net curtains

Use one of the many lovely net, lace, sheer or semi-sheer fabrics now in the shops to transform a bare window into a pretty and eye-catching room feature. Style the fabric into cross-over curtains, valanced curtains or a dramatic full-length drape.

Make pretty curtains from net, lace, sheer or semi-sheer fabric to dress a window in a kitchen, bathroom, hall or landing where heavier, drawn curtains are not always necessary. Use them in other rooms, too, during the summer when heavy curtains benefit from being cleaned and 'rested' away from the strong sunshine which fades and ages them.

Many styles of ready-made net curtains are now available in the shops, but making your own is economical and enables you to achieve a perfect fit for windows that are not a standard size. You also have a wider choice of fabric and can add trimmings to match your room scheme. Details of buying and sewing sheer fabrics, making a cased heading and how to care for net curtaining are given on pages 29 to 33. This chapter gives design ideas and making up instructions for three decorative styles of window dressing using these delicate fabrics. Choose from curtains with a combined valance, cross-over draped curtains or a simple but eye-catching draped valance over a decorative curtain pole.

Combined curtain and valance

A valance and lightweight side curtains sewn in one eliminates the need for two rods or wires and ensures a neater, less bulky heading. The curtains are gathered and fixed at the top so they cannot be drawn back and forth. Instead, they look very pretty draped to the sides and held with fabric or brass tie-backs which are easily released.

A separate strip of fabric joins the curtain and valance and forms the cased heading so the curtains can be hung on a decorative pole, simple rod or wire (see page 32).

Measuring up and cutting out

Cut a strip of fabric for the casing the length of the pole or the width of the window (whichever is the longer) plus side hem allowances. The depth of the strip must accommodate the wire or pole plus 1cm/½in seam allowance on each long side. Neaten the short side edges with narrow double hems if necessary.

Measure up and cut out the curtains in the usual way allowing at least 1½ times the window width for fullness, and sew side and lower edge hems. Trim the top of each curtain so that it will just reach the hanging rod. Run a row of gathering stitches 1cm/½in below this edge and pull up each curtain to exactly half the width of the casing strip. Tie the gathering threads securely and spread the gathers evenly over the width.

The depth of the valance is a matter of personal taste and varies according to the proportion of the window. Add 3cm/1¼in seam allowance to the required depth and allow approximately twice the width of the window for the width of the valance. Neaten the side edges with a narrow double hem (1cm/½in and 1cm/½in). Hem the bottom edge in a similar way or add a lace or frilled edging, trimming away any excess hem allowance. Omit hems if using selvedges. Run a gathering thread along the top edge of the valance and pull up to the width of the casing strip.

Making up the curtains and valance

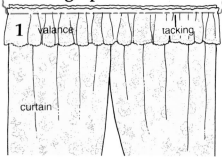

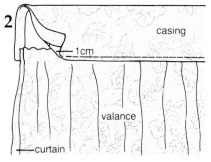

Lay the curtains out flat, right side up and with the two inside edges butted up together. Lay the valance across the two curtains, wrong side down, matching gathered edges.
1 Tack securely together along the top edge.

2 Turn 1cm/½in to the wrong side along all the edges of the casing strip and tack to hold. Fold the strip in half, lengthwise, wrong sides facing, and place over the top gathered edges of the curtain/ valance, overlapping it by 1cm/½in so that the raw edges are enclosed in the casing. Tack in place. Machine stitch the length of casing in place, sewing 5mm/⅜in from the edge through all layers – curtain, valance and both sides of the casing.

Remove all tacking, press well and thread on to a rod or wire to hang. Hold the curtains to the sides of the window with a simple tie-back. Choose from a length of silken cord (adding tassels to the ends), matching or contrasting ribbon or a length of delicately scalloped and embroidered broderie anglaise with the raw edge neatened. See pages 32, 33 and opposite for ideas.

Prettily draped cross-over curtains: the top edges can be overlapped either partially or completely.

Cross-over draped curtains

These are gathered up with the usual amount of fullness but are wide enough to overlap at the top so that while draped back to the sides of the window, forming attractive folds, they do not leave a large area of bare window.

The two curtains are sewn together at the top and hang on a single rod or wire, so they can't, of course, be drawn back and forth.

To maintain a straight lower edge on the curtain, the draped inside edge of each curtain requires a greater length of fabric than the straight outer edge. The hems are therefore angled.

Measuring up and cutting out

Allow at least 1½ times the window width for the width of *each* curtain.
1 Measure the length of the straight shorter outside edge from the hanging wire or rod to the window sill. To calculate the length of the longer inner edge, drape a tape measure from one end of the rod to a suitable tie-back point on the opposite side of the window and down to the window sill. Add the

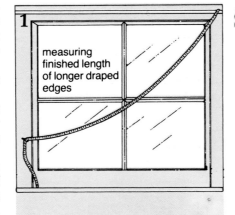

same allowance for the top casing and bottom hem to each of these measurements.

Cut both curtains to the longer length then lay right sides together and mark off the shorter length along one side. Cut diagonally across from this point to the opposite lower corner to angle the hem. This ensures that one curtain slopes in the reverse direction to the other.

Neaten side and lower edges with

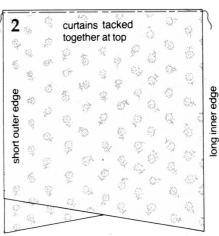

narrow double hems, adding a frill to the longer inside edges if required (see page 64).
2 With right sides upwards, lay one curtain on top of the other and tack the straight top edges together. Complete the heading, treating the two curtains as one, either adding a heading tape or making a casing. Hang the curtains and drape them back to the sides, holding them with fabric tie-backs or decorative curtain holders.

All-in-one valance and side curtains

The dramatic effect of this draped valance falling into side curtains is simply achieved by securing a long length of reversible lacy curtaining over a decorative curtain pole. This creative style of window dressing is pretty rather than practical and ideal as a replacement for heavier curtains during the summer.

Measuring up

To calculate the amount of fabric required, drape a tape measure (or a piece of string) from one end of the pole to the other, allowing it to droop in the curve you want for the valance. Add this measurement to the length needed for the side curtains (twice the height from floor to pole) plus hem allowances on both sides. This gives the length of fabric required.

If you are using a patterned fabric with a one-way design, the curtain will have to be cut in two so that the pattern will be upright on both sides. Add enough extra fabric to join two pieces together with a narrow French seam. The design should be level on both side curtains, so that the same part of the pattern lies at the lower edge on each, and you may also need to allow extra fabric for this.

Making up

As this type of curtain is not drawn across the window, one width of fabric is normally sufficient, and therefore side hems are unnecessary. Cut a fabric with a one way pattern in half across the width and join the top edges of the two halves with a narrow French seam so that the pattern will be upright on both side curtains. Neaten the lower edges with a narrow double hem, a pretty satin binding or with a lace or frilled edging.

Measure the length of the drop from each end and, with tailor's chalk, draw two lines across the width of the fabric to mark the central area allowed for the valance drape. Lay the fabric over the pole with the curtains falling behind and the valance in front of the pole. Adjust the fabric so that the two curtains hang well, then adjust and pin folds at both ends of the valance so that it falls in a pleasing way. Take down the curtains/valance carefully and secure the folds at each end of the valance with a few hand stitches. Remove pins and re-hang to check the final effect, adjusting if necessary. To prevent the fabric slipping off the pole, cut two 5cm/2in pieces of 'stick and sew' Velcro fastening. Stitch the sew-on halves of the Velcro to the ends of the valance on the wrong side, at a point where the fabric has been folded several times so that they will not show.

Replace the curtains/valance on the curtain pole and stick the self-adhesive halves of the Velcro to the pole to correspond with the sewn on halves. Add extra Velcro if the valance shows a tendency to slip.

Below: Lengths of border-patterned Terylene net create a strikingly pretty window dressing.

Curtain heading tapes and detachable linings

All curtains, with the exception of sheers and curtains with a deliberately delicate look, gain from a lining. Adding a lining will cost you more in money and effort, but the curtains will hang better, look more professional and provide valuable insulation.

Curtains shut out the dark, protect the sleeper from the dawn and give privacy. A lining acts as a barrier between the curtain and window and fulfils several vital functions:
– it cuts down light penetration through the curtain fabric (especially important in bedrooms)
– it provides insulation, helping to cut down on draughts and cold air from the windows
– it weighs down the curtain, giving it more 'body' and a better hang
– it protects the curtain fabric from the damaging effects of sunlight, and to some extent from dirt and dust

– a detachable lining can be removed for separate laundering
– on really draughty windows where one lining is not enough, an inter-lining of a fine blanket-like material sewn to the curtain fabric before the lining is attached gives a further layer of insulation. Interlinings are dealt with on page 48.
The fabric generally sold as curtain lining' is 100% cotton. The weave is close and dense to cut out light and draughts. Thermal curtain-lining fabric, which has a special coating on one side, is a little more expensive to buy, but provides extra insulation.

Choosing the lining method

There are several ways to line curtains. Which method you choose depends on the size of the curtain and the weight of the fabric and, of course, your personal preference.

Detachable linings are suitable if the curtain and lining fabric have different laundering requirements, or if you want to add a lining to an existing unlined curtain. The curtain and lining are completely separate and just held together at the top by virtue of sharing the same curtain hooks.

Sewn-in linings are suitable for small or lightweight curtains. They are joined to the curtain down the side hems and across the top. They are covered in the next chapter.

Locked-in linings are suitable for large or weighty curtains. In addition to being attached to the curtain across the top and down the sides, the lining is invisibly lock-stitched to the curtain fabric at regular intervals from top to bottom over the whole curtain. Locked-in linings are dealt with on pages 46-47.

Below: The lining in these curtains gives them extra body and a good hang.

Creating a heading for your curtain

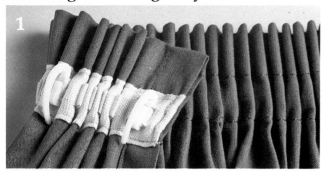

The easiest way to create a decorative heading is to use a ready-made curtain heading tape. This has cords running through it to pull both tape and fabric up into gathers or pleats, and pockets for hanging hooks.
The basic heading styles are:
1 Even gathering
2 Pencil pleating
3 Triple pleating
4 Cylindrical pleating
There are other tapes which create different visual effects, but they are less widely available. If you do use tapes other than the four styles above, follow the manufacturers' instructions for the amount of tape and fabric needed and attaching method. Hand-made headings – hard work

but very professional-looking – are dealt with on pages 50-53.

How much fabric?

The type of heading you use determines the amount of fabric needed for both curtains and lining, so choosing a heading should be your first consideration. A gathered heading needs only 1½ times the track width of fabric, although up to 3 times can be used for sheers. Pencil pleats need 2¼ to 2½ times and triple and cylindrical pleats twice the track width.

How much tape?

You need as much tape as the finished flat width of each curtain

plus an extra amount for accurate placing of the pleats and neatening. Check with the shop assistant how much you need – for triple pleating allow 30cm/12in extra per curtain.

Which heading?

The type of heading you choose depends on the look you want. Each style of heading tape shown is suitable for any weight of fabric, but there are some general guidelines to follow.
For short curtains the shallower tapes such as 'Rufflette' brand gathered tape, pencil pleating, triple pleating and cylindrical pleating look best. A deep heading tape might look top-heavy on a short curtain.

Pencil pleating

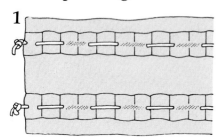

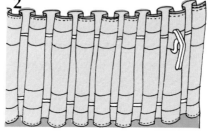

For each curtain, cut a piece of tape to the curtain width plus at least 7cm/2¾in for neatening edges.
1 At the edge of the tape which will be at the centre, pull 4cm/1½in of cords free and knot. Trim surplus tape to within 5mm/¼in of knots and turn edge to wrong side. (The right side of the tape has pockets.) At the other end, pull 5cm/2in of cords free and turn tape to wrong side. Place wrong side of tape to wrong side of curtain 3mm/⅛in down from the top edge with the tape the correct way up. (Rufflette brand tape has a yellow line at the bottom.) If you are not sure which way up the tape should be, insert

hooks and check the hang on your track. Tack the tape to the curtain 3mm/⅛in in from each long edge and, from the wrong side of the curtain, machine the tape each side in the same direction. Machine both short edges, taking care not to stitch across loose cords. Hold cords, pull up fabric to maximum pleating, then ease to correct width.
2 Knot the cords to secure, and insert hooks at either end and at about 8cm/3in intervals along the tape. (With Rufflette Regis, use R40 hooks) If you want the curtain to cover the track, add hooks to the bottom row of pockets. If you want it to hang below, use the top row.

Triple pleating

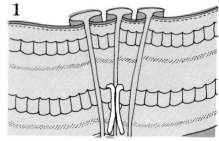

At the edge of the tape which will be at the centre, cut across the first pleat to free the cords. Knot each cord and trim surplus tape to 5mm/¼in. If the curtain tracks overlap turn 4cm/1½in of tape to the wrong side of this centre edge. If the curtains are to butt up, turn 9cm/3½in. The amount of tape turned back on the centre edge governs the pleat position. Neaten this edge and cut tape to fit curtain width allowing at least 6cm/2¼in at the outer edge for neatening. Free 5cm/2in of the cords from outer edge, free from tape with scissors point. Trim off surplus tape to within 5mm/¼in of cords and fold to

For long curtains extra-deep versions of pencil and triple pleating give the best proportioned look, but standard depth tapes can also be used if preferred. With sheer fabrics, even a simple gathered tape gives a neat heading on long curtains.

Fabric choice and laundering

Curtain tapes are suitable for any weight or type of fabric and are washable and dry cleanable, so you should launder curtains according to the washing instructions of your curtain fabric. Use the lowest heat when ironing synthetic fibre tapes.

Which curtain track?

Which curtain track you use depends on whether you want the curtain to conceal it (as in most plastic tracking), or to be suspended below. Poles fall into this second category.

Some tapes such as Rufflette brand gathered (Standard), pencil pleating (Regis), triple pleating (Tridis) and cylindrical pleating (Cartridge) have hook pockets positioned so that they can be used with either type of hanging. Deep triple pleating (Deep Tridis) and deeper pencil pleating (Deep Regis) are manufactured in two versions, one for covering the track, the other for a suspended heading.

How to attach a heading tape

The easiest tape to sew to a curtain head is gathered tape (see page 28).

Above: The photographs show,
1 gathered heading (Rufflette Standard),
2 pencil pleating (Rufflette Regis),
3 triple pleating (Rufflette Tridis) and
4 cylindrical pleating (Rufflette Cartridge).

For pencil, triple or cylindrical pleating tape, turn a minimum hem allowance of 6mm/¼in at the top of curtain to the wrong side and press. When attaching tape, be careful to knot the cords on the correct end of the curtain, depending on whether it is to be hung on the left or on the right. The cord ends are knotted and turned to the wrong side on the centre edges of each curtain. Never cut off surplus cords at outer edges.

Cylindrical pleating

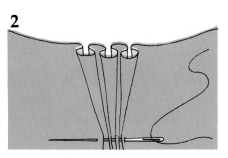

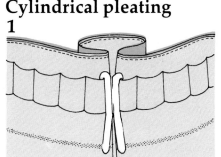

wrong side.
Sew in place as for pencil pleating. Pull the cords and push up the tape and fabric to form the first set of pleats. Move along, forming pleats and tie a slip knot with the cords.
1 This style of tape needs a two-pronged hook (Rufflette R10). One hook is inserted behind each pleat set, each prong into an adjacent pocket. Add a hook at both the centre and outer edge. Use the bottom pockets for covering the track, the top for suspending the curtain.
2 To keep the pleats tight, a small neat tack can be sewn through the base of the front of each pleat.

At the edge of the tape which will be at the centre, cut across the first pleat to free the cords. Knot each cord and cut tape to within 5mm/¼in of knots.
If your two curtain tracks overlap, turn 2.5cm/1in to wrong side of this centre edge. If the curtains are to butt up, turn 5cm/2in to neaten. Cut the tape to fit the curtain width allowing at least 6cm/2¼in at the outer edge for neatening. Free 5cm/2in of the cords from outer edge, picking cords out with a scissor point if they are not visible. Trim tape to within 5mm/¼in of cords. Attach tape as for pencil pleating.

Hold the cords and push the tape up into pleats, keeping each pleat tight. Tie a slip knot to secure cords.
1 The same hooks are used as for the triple pleating, one for each pleat and one at each end, placed in the bottom row of pockets for covering the track or the top row for suspending.
2 For extra pleat definition, each pleat can be stuffed with rolled-up tissue paper.

Making a detachable lining

Detachable linings are the simplest of all to make. These completely separate linings are attached to the main curtains by sharing the same curtain hooks.

The main advantage of a detachable lining is that the curtain and lining can be laundered separately. This could be useful if the fabric and lining have different laundering requirements – in some cases the lining may be dry cleanable only (as with thermal lining material) and the curtain fabric washable, or vice-versa.

Even if both the curtain and lining are washable, the combined weight of both sewn together often makes the curtain a very heavy and bulky item to wash by hand. If the curtain is large it may be too bulky to fit in a domestic washing machine. A detachable lining which can be separated from the curtain reduces this bulk.

A special heading tape is available for detachable linings. It is designed to be used in conjunction with a heading tape on the curtain sharing the same hooks. Some curtain tracks have combined hooks and gliders with an additional ring for hooking on a lining.

Detachable linings use less fabric than sewn-in linings since, whichever type of heading is on the curtain, only 1½ times the track width in lining is necessary.

This type of lining can easily be added to existing unlined curtains.

Measure up and cut out the main fabric and lining, using the same

Above: A strip of contrast fabric sewn to the inner edge and bottom of each curtain accentuates the draped shape. Instructions for making contrast fabric borders are given on pages 64-65. The pleated tie-back is shown opposite.

basic method as for unlined curtains (see page 26), but allowing sufficient fabric width for the heading of your choice.

Make up the main curtain in exactly the same way as for an unlined curtain, attaching the heading tape of your choice.

Make up the lining as for an unlined curtain, but leave the top as a raw edge and attach lining heading tape to this raw edge as described in the instructions (right).

Attaching lining heading tape

1

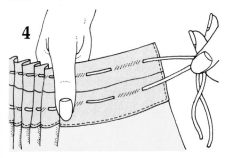

This tape (Rufflette brand) is made up of two 'skirts', one skirt fitting each side of the top of the lining fabric.

The right side of the tape is the corded side.

Remember to make a left and right-hand version for a pair of curtains.

Cut a length of lining tape to the width of the curtain plus at least 10cm/4in for neatening the ends.

2

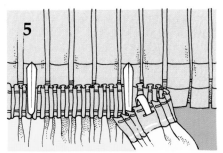

1cm

1 At the end of the tape that will be at the centre, pull the two cords free and secure with a knot. Trim off surplus tape up to the knot.

2 Ease the two skirts apart and slip the top of the lining between the skirts, with the corded side on the right side of the lining.

Place the knotted end at the centre edge of the curtain lining, overhanging the end of the lining

3

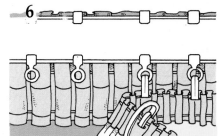

by 1cm/½in.

Turn 5mm/¼in and then remaining 5mm/¼in at knotted end of tape to wrong side of lining. Pin tape in place.

At outer edge of tape, pull 4cm/1½in of each cord free and trim surplus tape so that it overhangs lining by 1cm/½in. Neaten with a double hem 5mm/¼in and 5mm/¼in to wrong side of lining, leaving the

4

loose cords free for gathering up. Tack tape in place.

3 Stitch tape in place, close to the bottom edge and down both sides, being sure not to catch the loose ends of the cords into the stitching. Remove tacking.

4 Hold the two cord ends and gently pull the cords at the same time as pushing up the fabric and

5

tape until the fabric is fully gathered. Now ease out the gathers until the lining is the required fullness for the curtain.

5 Insert curtain hooks, spacing evenly at about every 8cm/3in through slits on top of the lining tape. With wrong side of lining and wrong side of curtain facing, fit the hooks through the pockets on the

6

curtain heading tape, so that both lining and curtain hang from the same hooks.

6 For curtain tracks that have combined hook/gliders with rings for lining hooks, the lining tape should be fitted with hooks which then fit through the rings under the main curtain hooks.

Pleated curtain tie-back

This is a quick and simple way to make a professional looking pleated tie-back using curtain heading tape. The most suitable style of tape to use is pencil pleating, either Rufflette Regis (7.5cm/3in deep) or Deep Regis (13.8cm/5½in).

Measure round the full bulk of the pulled back curtain and lining. Cut fabric to 2½ times this length plus 3cm/1¼in and to same depth as the heading tape plus 3cm/1¼in. Cut tape the same

length.

All round the fabric, turn 1cm/½in to wrong side and tack. Centre tape on wrong side of fabric. Neaten the short ends of the tape as for a curtain head. Stitch tape in place and pull up to pleat. To hold the two ends of the tie-back together, sew a ring to each end on the wrong sides. Slot the rings onto a hook screwed into the wall, positioned so that the tie-back holds the curtain in a generous drape.

DESIGN EXTRA

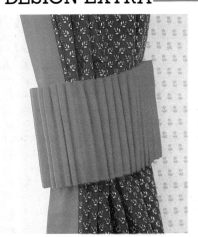

Sewn-in curtain linings for a permanent finish

If your curtain fabric and lining can be laundered together, the sewn-in method of curtain lining is ideal. Its advantage is that it gives you a neat finish down the side hems and across the top. The hem of the lining is left free from the curtain for the best possible hang.

With this method, curtains and lining are attached by being sewn together down the side hems and across the top. Both long and short curtains can be lined like this.

Before reading this chapter read through pages 26-28 and 37-39 for basic curtain making techniques.

Long, heavy curtains are best lined by the locked-in method which secures curtain and lining with vertical lines of stitching (see pages 46-47).

Measuring up and cutting out

Calculate the amount of fabric needed for each curtain using the same basic method as for unlined curtains, but allowing sufficient fabric width for the heading of your choice. Measure up for the lining fabric in exactly the same way as for the curtain fabric, but cut the lining fabric to 1cm/½in less than the *finished* width of curtain, and do not add the hem allowance at the top. The top hem allowance on the curtain is 4cm/1½in for gathered heading tape and a minimum of 6mm/¼in for other heading tapes (including gathered tape when used as a suspended heading).

Right: A pleated frill on these bedroom curtains gives them a soft, but not too feminine, designer touch.

Making a sewn-in curtain lining

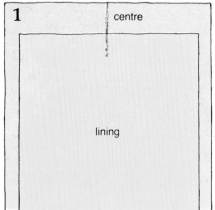

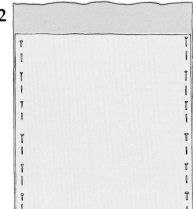

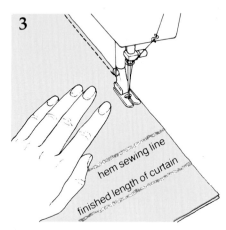

With flat seams, join the curtain fabric widths together to make up each curtain, and join the lining fabric widths to make up each lining. Fell or French seams are not necessary since the edges of the flat seam will be hidden between the lining and the curtain.

1 Mark the centre point on the wrong side of both the curtain fabric and the lining with tailor's chalk.

2 Position lining on curtain fabric, right sides facing with top of lining 4cm/1½in (or hem allowance) below the curtain fabric. Pin the raw edges together down both sides. You will find that the curtain fabric is wider than the lining, so allow the curtain fabric to form a few gentle folds in order to match the raw edges exactly.

Measuring from the top of the lining fabric (ie, the top of the lining fabric (ie, the top of the finished curtain), mark the curtain length required with tailor's chalk on to both the lining and the curtain fabric. Also mark the position of the hem. The hem allowance for the bottom edge is generally 15cm/6in, 1cm/½in being turned under first, followed by 14cm/5½in.

3 Sew both side seams with a 1cm/½in seam, sewing from the top of the lining to within 10cm/4in of the hem sewing line.

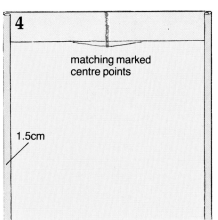

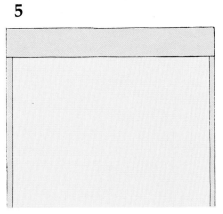

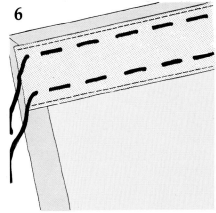

4 Turn curtain fabric and lining through to the right side. Press lining and curtain fabric flat, matching the centre marked points on lining and fabric. The curtain fabric overlaps on the lining side by 1.5cm/⅝in down each side edge.

5 Turn curtain fabric to the lining side at the top of the curtain, folding along the top edge of the lining.

6 Attach heading tape to the top of

the curtain, covering the raw edge. Turn up a double hem on the bottom of the curtain fabric. Tack in place.

For extra neatness and less bulk on the corners you can mitre each corner.

Turn up a double hem to the wrong side on the lining fabric, so that the lining hangs about 2cm/¾in above hem level of curtain fabric. The depth of the lining hem should be

the same as, or less than, the curtain fabric hem, so you will have to trim off the surplus lining fabric to make the hem to the correct depth. Tack hem in place.

Pull up the heading tape to make the curtains the correct width for the window. Hang the curtains in place for several days to give the fabric time to 'drop'. Adjust the hems if necessary and then slipstitch.

Mock mitres on hem corners

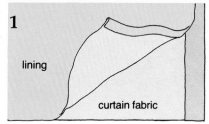

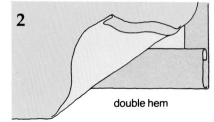

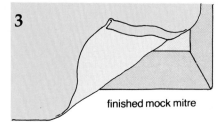

A mitred corner makes a neat finish on a curtain hem. A true mitre should be a 45° angle, but with curtains, the bottom hem is deeper than the side hems and a mock mitre is by far the simplest method.

To make this mock mitred corner you have to cheat with the angle

of the mitre. Only one side of the corner (the deeper bottom hem side) is mitred, and this is not at a 45° angle.

The lining and the curtain fabric are sewn together to within 10cm/4in of the hem sewing line (see page 42).

1 Turn in and press the

remaining side hem allowance on the curtain fabric.

2 Turn up a double hem at the bottom.

3 Fold the bottom hem allowance under at an angle on the corner until its top edge touches the side hem allowance. Sew in place with slipstitches.

Matching patterned fabrics

When working with patterned fabric, take care to match the pattern correctly along each seam. On the selvedge edge of the fabric, measure the distance between one pattern and the next identical one. This is called the 'pattern repeat' and you will often see it quoted on furnishing fabric details. You need to know the length of the pattern repeat when you are measuring up for curtains as you must buy extra fabric for matching the pattern. Unless you are making curtains for a very narrow window, each curtain will be made up of more than one width of fabric. With a patterned fabric, the pattern must be matched at each seam and also at the centre of a pair of curtains where they join when closed.

1 Before cutting your first piece of curtain fabric, make sure the end is cut exactly straight (at right angles to the sides.) With tailor's chalk mark a line across the width to

indicate the top hem allowance. For the best effect, you need to show the complete pattern, or a representative proportion of it, along the top edge of the curtain. If your tailor's chalk line intersects the pattern at a visually unbalanced point (perhaps cutting through a flower pattern so that the heads would be turned to the wrong side for hem allowance and stalks left at the top of the curtain) then alter the top hem allowance. Re-position the tailor's chalk line and cut off any surplus fabric to leave just the hem allowance.

2 Cut this first piece of fabric to the required length (drop of curtain plus top and bottom hems) and lay right side up on a large table or on the floor. Lay out the rest of the fabric, right side upwards, and match the pattern to the first cut piece.

Cut the second piece of fabric so that you have two identical pieces.

Right: Even if you are making up curtains in a small overall pattern like this design, it's important to match the pattern when cutting out the fabric widths and when seaming them together.

Continue in this way until you have cut all the required fabric pieces.

To seam two pieces together
Mark the centre of each pattern repeat on the fabric selvedges (or the cut side edges) with a pin. Lay the two pieces of fabric, right sides facing, matching the pins in the selvedge edges, and pin along the seamline. Turn the fabric to the right side and check that the pattern is matching exactly – make adjustments if necessary.

Tack along the seamline. Remove all pins and then turn the fabric to the right side and check again that the pattern is matching. Sew the seam and remove tacking.

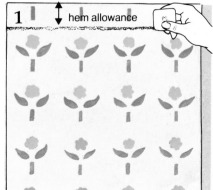

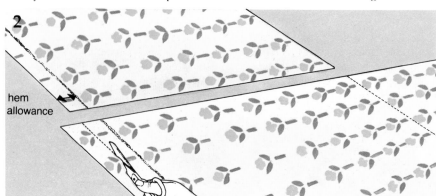

Pleated perfection

A pleated curtain frill gives a soft designer look to curtains used in any room.

Cut the curtain lining as for a sewn-in lining, but to the same width as the curtain fabric.

To calculate the fabric needed for the pleated frill, double the finished frill width (say 6cm/2¼in) and add 5cm/2in (ie total width of 17cm/6½in). For length allow three times the finished curtain drop and add 3cm/1¼in. Wrong sides facing, fold the fabric in half along its length. Make pleats in either box pleat style (below left) or side pleat style (below right), by marking the pleat spacings with tailor's chalk down the frill fabric and folding and tacking in place.

Neaten the top short edge with a 5mm/¼in and 1cm/½in double hem.

1 Place frill to right side of curtain, matching raw edges and with neatened short edge to finished top of curtain. Cut off any left-over trim at hemline and neaten the edge. Tack in place.

2 Lay lining fabric right sides facing to curtain fabric, matching raw edges and sew both side hems taking 2.5cm/1in seams. Continue making up as for sewn-in linings.

If you have a ruffler attachment for your machine, you can use this to make side pleats quickly from a single fabric thickness. Use half the frill width, and neaten the frill edge with a double hem.

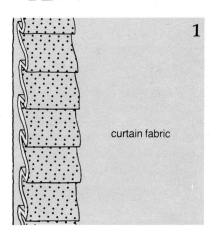

curtain fabric

1

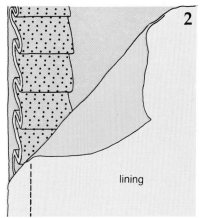

lining

2

box pleats

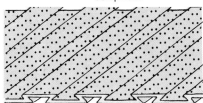

side pleats

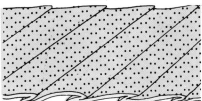

Locked-in and decorative linings and interlining

Locked-in linings give a really professional look to large curtains and help them to hang beautifully.
Add interlining for an even more luxurious touch or a thermal lining for extra insulation. Alternatively, turn the lining itself into a decorative feature.

Curtain linings no longer have to be dull beige sateen. They are now available in a wide range of colours and even thermal lining, coated with a layer of insulating material, can be silvery white or rich cream, as well as beige.

Locked-in linings help to give large curtains a really professional finish. For ultra-elegant curtains, add inter-

Above: Wide curtains often suffer from bunched up linings but with the lining locked-in they hang beautifully.

lining as well. This helps curtains to look luxuriously thick and to drape well, and will insulate windows almost as effectively as double glazing.

There is no real reason why a closely-woven dress print or furnishing cotton should not be used as a lining. The extra expense is justified by the decorative effect. Reveal the lining by making it into a decorative border or simply drape the curtain back attractively. Follow one of these two ways of showing off decorative linings for an attractive window treatment.

Curtains with locked-in linings

Locking is a means of joining curtain fabric and lining together at intervals down the length. Held against the lining in this way, the fabric of large, wide or heavy curtains drapes well and falls in graceful folds. Lining also protects the fabric from direct sunlight and dust, and provides more effective insulation.

Cutting out
Measure and cut out curtain fabric as for unlined curtains (see page 26), allowing sufficient width for the heading and adding 4cm/1½in top hem, 10cm/4in bottom hem, 4cm/1½in for each side hem and 3cm/1¼in for each seam joining fabric widths, if necessary. Cut lining to the same width, joining widths if necessary, but to the *finished* curtain length.

Right: Locking in the lining.

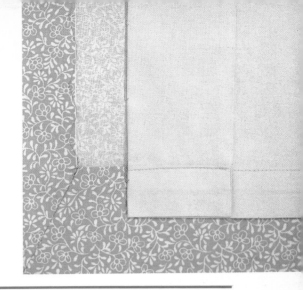

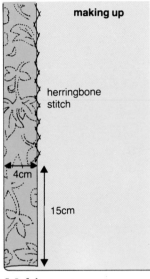

making up

herringbone stitch

4cm

15cm

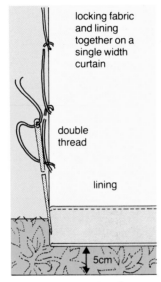

locking fabric and lining together on a single width curtain

double thread

lining

5cm

locking seams together on a wider curtain

lining

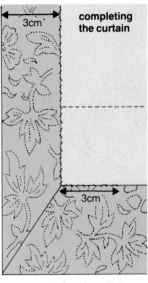

3cm

completing the curtain

3cm

Making up
Press a 4cm/1½in turning to the wrong side down each side of the curtain, making sure it is straight with the grain.
Herringbone stitch down these edges using a large stitch and picking up just a thread on the main fabric so the stitches will not show on the right side. End stitching about 15cm/6in above lower edge to allow for hem.
Turn up and press a 10cm/4in bottom hem, making sure it is absolutely straight. Fold into a mock mitre in the corners (see page 44). Fold in 2cm/¾in along the top edge of hem, then tack and slipstitch down taking care not to make stitches noticeable on the right side of curtain.
Make a hem along the bottom edge of lining, turning 1.5cm/⅝in then 3.5cm/1⅜in to the wrong side, and machine or hand stitch.

Locking together
Lay curtain fabric out flat, right side down, on a large table or the floor.

Place the lining on top, wrong side down, with the lower edge 5cm/2in above lower edge of curtain.
On a single width curtain fold back one third of the lining, aligning top and bottom edges to make sure the fold is straight and smoothing it down with your fingertips.
Using double thread and working from right to left, pick up two threads on the lining and then the same on the curtain fabric. Leave a loop of thread running along for about 10cm/4in, then again pick up a thread or two in the lining and fabric, bringing the needle out into the loop of thread like a large blanket stitch. Continue working along the length of the curtain in this way, leaving the thread fairly loose so that it does not pull on the fabric.
Fold the lining back over the fabric and smooth flat, then fold back a third of the lining on the other long side and stitch in the same way.
On a wider curtain, the seams should be locked together and further lines of locking stitches

made at approximately 40cm/16in intervals (dividing each width into thirds). Begin at the seam nearest to the centre of the curtain, folding back the lining and stitching as above, and work outwards from this. When locking two seams together, stitch through the seam allowances only so no stitches have to be made on the main fabric of curtain or lining.

Completing the curtain
Trim the lining width so the edges are even with the curtain edges then turn in 3cm/1in down each side of lining. Tack the lining down without stretching it, then neatly slipstitch it to the folded-in edge of the curtain. Remove tacking, then slipstitch lining around each lower corner for about 3cm/1¼in leaving the remaining hemmed edges free. Measure the required length from bottom to top at intervals and turn in the top hem. Press and tack down, then attach the heading tape, covering the raw edge in the usual way.

Curtains with interlining and linings

An interlining adds a luxurious, almost padded effect to curtains, as well as providing effective window insulation. Most curtain fabrics can be interlined except, of course, sheers and nets.

The most popular interlining is a brushed cotton, which resembles a thin fluffy blanket. A domette is a finer, fluffy fabric suitable for interlining more delicate curtaining. There are also synthetic versions which drape very well but do not help to block out the light.

Interlined curtains are an extension of curtains with locked-in linings, so read those instructions first.

Cutting out

Cut out and join widths of curtain fabric and lining. Cut out interlining to the same size as curtain fabric.

Making up

To join widths of interlining, butt the edges together, or very slightly overlap them, and oversew or herringbone stitch to hold. You can join with a zigzag machine stitch, but take care not to stretch the interlining in doing this.

Spread the interlining out flat on a table or the floor and lay the curtain fabric, wrong side down, on top, smoothing it out evenly all over. Fold back the fabric and lock it to the interlining, as for locking in linings. Stitch two rows of locking on each width of fabric and a row on each seam.

When the locking is complete, smooth down the fabric over the interlining and tack the two together all round the edge.

Turn the curtain over so that the interlining is uppermost, fold in a 4cm/1½in turning down each side and herringbone down. Fold up a 10cm/4in single thickness bottom hem, mitring corners, and herringbone this to the interlining.

Adding lining

Do not make a hem on the lining but lay it right side up on the interlined side of curtain with side and bottom edges together. Lock the lining to the interlining and complete curtain as before except along the lower edge of lining, which should be turned in and slipstitched down as for the side edges.

a selection of curtain linings and interlinings

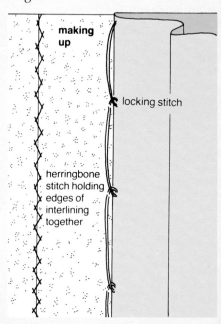

making up

locking stitch

herringbone stitch holding edges of interlining together

Curtains with lining borders

A very attractive way of showing off a decorative lining is to use it to form a border down each side of the curtain. This does not involve any extra work when making up curtains by the sewn-in lining method, as it is simply a reversal of the normal procedure of wrapping the fabric on to the lining side.

Whether it is plain or patterned, toning or contrasting, choose your lining carefully so that it highlights the curtain fabric. Use a pretty print to enliven plain curtains, or frame a geometric or floral pattern with a plain border in a strong colour.

Making up

Follow the instructions on pages 42-43 for curtains with sewn-in linings, but cut the *lining* rather than the curtain fabric to the larger size. For a 5cm/2in border down each side of the curtain, cut the lining 10cm/4in wider than the curtain fabric. Make up the curtains in the normal way but press them so that a strip of lining forms a border down each side edge before completing top edge and finishing the bottom hem.

Diagonal draping

Turn simple curtains into an unusual and decorative room feature by using a pretty or eye-catching fabric rather than a plain lining fabric and draping back the curtain corners to reveal it. Choose the lining to complement your curtains and perhaps to bring a splash of colour or an interesting pattern into the room. Adapt the idea to give a fresh new look to existing but rather dull curtains or economise by using old but attractive curtains as the lining fabric for a new pair.

The method of making up is extremely simple but the two fabrics must be compatible, needing the same type of cleaning and care, and both must be pre-shrunk as you will not have a hem to let down. You will need the same amount of lining as curtain fabric.

Making up

Measure up (see page 26) and cut curtain fabric and lining to exactly the same size, joining widths if necessary.

Place the curtain fabric and lining right sides together and stitch round three sides, leaving the top edge open. Clip off corners of seam allowance, turn right side out and press well. Turn the top edge over to the lining side and lay the curtain heading tape in position, covering raw edges. Machine stitch in place.

Gather up the top to required width and hang the curtains, then sew a small brass ring to the sides or lower corners. Fold back the curtain edges to reveal the lining and mark the appropriate position on the wall behind each curtain for a hook. Screw in a small brass hook at each side and hook the ring over this to hold curtain in place. At night, simply slip the ring off the hook so the windows can be completely covered.

Below: A stunning flower print adds an eye-catching touch to plain curtains. The higher the rings are placed, the more lining is revealed.

Hand-made pleated headings for professional-looking curtains

Give curtains a really special, custom-made look with hand-stitched, pinch-pleat headings. Follow the professional method of making triple or goblet pleats, rather than using tape, to create fuller, more graceful curtains with perfectly-positioned pleats.

When you have splashed out on a luxurious and expensive fabric to make really special curtains, add the ultimate professional finish with a hand-stitched heading.

Although more time-consuming than using commercial heading tape, making pinch pleats by hand enables you to choose the exact depth of pleat that suits the proportions of your curtains or of a printed fabric design.

By being able to put more fullness in the pleats and spacing them more closely, you can make fuller curtains which will hang more gracefully. Hand-made curtains also have a softer appearance as there are no lines of machine stitching running across the top. And adding this exclusive finish may cost less than ready-made tape.

Left: Curtains with goblet pleated headings fall into graceful folds.

Types of pinch pleating

Triple pleats are the most popular form of pinch pleated heading, but goblet pleats provide an unusual variation and are even easier to make. Being one of the few styles of curtain heading that – as yet – it is not possible to create with commercial heading tape, goblet pleating invariably adds a very unusual, custom-made finish to your curtains.

The pinch pleat method can also be adapted to make a valance with clusters of pleats (they can be groups of four or five pleats – not necessarily three) spaced irregularly or more widely than usual, to echo vertical window divisions or just to add an individual touch.

Buying materials

The only items needed to make curtains with hand-stitched headings –

apart from the curtain fabric, lining and possibly interlining – are some stiffening and hooks. White, buckram-type stiffenings made specifically for curtain headings in suitable widths are widely available. Select a width about 2cm/¾in greater than the required depth of pleat. Choose either steel pin hooks that simply slip behind the pleat stitching or traditional brass sew-on hooks.

You will need

Curtain fabric
Matching thread
Lining fabric
Interlining if used
Curtain buckram slightly deeper than required heading pleats, twice width of flat curtain
Pronged steel hooks or sew-on hooks and strong thread (1 hook for each pleat plus 4 for edges)

Measuring up and preparing the curtains

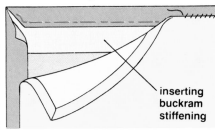

inserting buckram stiffening

Measure up as described on page 26, adding 14cm/5½in to the finished length for top and bottom hems.

For triple pleats, the width of each curtain should be two and a half times the width of half the curtain rail, which allows 10-17cm/4½-6in for each pleat, depending on the spaces between, and creates luxuriously full curtains.

For goblet pleats, twice the width is sufficient. Allow 4cm/1½in for each

side hem, and 3cm/1¼in for each seam joining fabric widths, if necessary.

Cut out the curtains, joining widths as necessary. Cut lining to finished size of curtains and lock to prepared curtains (see page 47) but without stitching over heading area.

Inserting buckram stiffening Fold back top edge of lining and slip buckram underneath turnings of curtain fabric, trimming to fit, so that edges of buckram lie level with top and sides of curtain. Tack stiffening securely in place and re-position lining on top, smoothing it down.

Turn in top raw edge of lining to lie about 1cm/½in below top edge of curtain and slipstitch down taking care not to let stitches go through front of curtain.

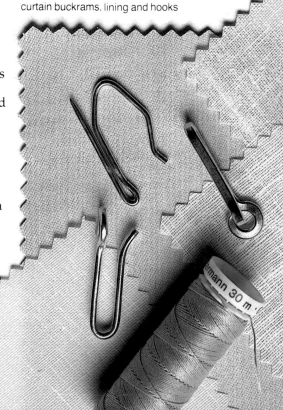

curtain buckrams. lining and hooks

Calculating pleat sizes

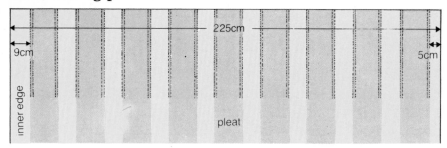

To ensure a perfect finish, spend some time calculating the size and spacing.

Number of pleats
Measure the required finished width of each curtain (half rail length) and, at each end, subtract 5cm/2in or the width of any overlap or return. Assuming a rough average figure of a triple pleat every 10cm/4in of finished curtain, calculate the number of pleats that will fit this width, with a pleat positioned at either end.

Example
Width of finished curtain (half track length)	90cm
Overlap at inner edge	9cm
Flat area at outer edge	5cm
Distance between first and last pleat	76cm
Number of pleats	9

Size of each pleat
From the width of the *flat* curtain, subtract the size of the *finished* curtain (including overlap) to calculate the amount of fabric left over for pleats. Divide this measurement by the required number of pleats to find the amount of fabric allowed for *each* pleat.

Example
Width of flat curtain	225cm
Width of finished curtain	90cm
Difference to be taken up in pleats	135cm
Number of pleats	9
Fabric for each pleat = 135 ÷ 9 =	15cm

Size of each space
To calculate the exact size of the spaces between pleats, divide the finished curtain width (less the return, overlap or 5cm/2in at each end) by the number of pleats less one.

Example
Width of finished curtain	90cm
Less 5cm one end and 9cm overlap other end	76cm
Number of pleats less one	8
Size of each space = 76cm ÷ 8 =	9.5cm

Making a goblet pleated heading

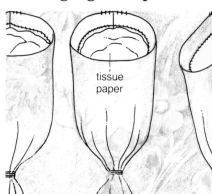

An unusual variation of pinch pleats, goblet pleats have the advantage of requiring slightly less width of fabric than triple pleats.

Calculating pleat sizes
Allowing 9-13cm/3½-5in for each goblet pleat and about the same amount for each space, calculate exact sizes as above.

If your flat curtain is exactly twice the finished size and there is no overlap or return, simply divide the flat width by an even number of pleats and spaces, for example, a 120cm/48in curtain would have twelve 10cm/4in pleats/spaces; that is six pleats, five whole spaces and a half space at either end.

Forming the goblet pleats
Mark out and stitch each pleat as for triple pleated headings (Step 1) as far as stitching from top edge to bottom of stiffening at each pleat. Instead of forming three pleats, pinch together the base of each pleat (folding the fabric into three or

Making a triple pleated heading

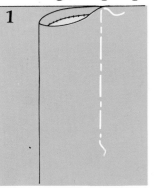 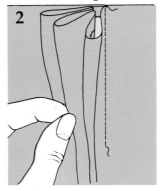 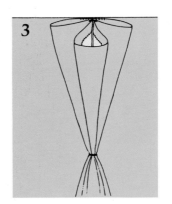 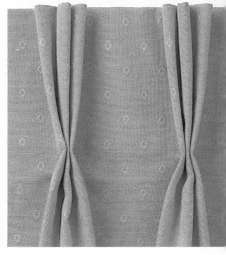

Calculate the exact size of spaces and pleats (see left) and then, using tailor's chalk and a ruler or set square, draw vertical lines to mark their position along the top edge of the curtains.

1 Bring together the two lines marking the first pleat, wrong sides of curtain facing, to form a single large pleat. Tack and stitch (by machine or by hand) from top edge of curtain to lower edge of stiffening, making sure that stitching is at a true right angle to curtain edge.

Repeat for each pleat: each curtain should then be the required finished width (half track length).

2 Hold the centre fold of each pleat between thumb and forefinger just above lower edge of stiffening, and push pleat inwards towards the stitching line, forming three small, evenly sized pleats. Catch the pleats together with a few small handstitches just above lower edge of stiffening.

3 At the top edge of curtain, catch the triple pleats together at the back and also anchor the back edge of the a few unobtrusive hand stitches using matching thread.

four small pleats) and catch the folds together with a few hand stitches at the base only.

To form the goblet shape, round out the top of each pleat and catch to the top edge of curtain about 1cm/½in out, on either side, from the first stitching line. To ensure that the goblet shape stays nicely rounded, lightly stuff each pleat with a piece of crumpled tissue paper. (Don't forget to remove this when cleaning curtains.)

Attaching hooks

If curtains are to hang just below a decorative wooden pole, attach the curtain hooks as close to the top edge as possible without protruding. If the curtain heading is to cover the rail, position the hooks lower down, according to depth of rail and style of gliders.

If using sew on hooks, attach one at each end of each curtain and one behind each pleat, stitching on very securely with strong button thread. If using pronged hooks, insert behind the stitching at each pleat. Insert the corner hooks by making two vertical rows of stitching at each end of curtains and inserting a hook between the rows.

PROFESSIONAL TOUCH

'Dressing' curtains

All curtains, whether or not their headings are made by hand, will drape more effectively if they are properly 'dressed'. To do this, hang the curtains half drawn open. Starting from the top, run your fingers down the curtain emphasizing each natural fold made by the heading. If necessary, a gentle tug on the lower hem edge, level with a heading pleat, will help the fabric fall into a natural pleat. Start from the outer edge and work along each curtain, drawing back the curtain as you create the draping.

If the curtain heading hangs below a decorative pole, push each space between pleats backwards. If the curtain covers the track, pull the space areas of fabric forwards.

When the curtains are fully drawn back into perfectly-draped folds, tie three lengths of cord or strips of soft fabric around each curtain and leave for as long as possible – at least overnight or preferably two or three days – to 'train' the pleats.

When the cords are removed, the curtains will retain the beautifully draped effect and will 'hang' well for quite some time, but repeat when re-hanging curtains after cleaning.

Traditional fabric pelmets

Custom-made to suit the proportions of your window and the styling of your room, traditional pelmets can be expensive to buy. With modern materials, however, they are simple to make yourself, cost very little, and add the same distinctive finish to your windows.

Pelmets are horizontal panels of stiffened fabric which, positioned at the top of curtains, cover curtain track and balance the proportions of a window. They are particularly attractive on tall windows and are also effective when used to link together adjoining sets of windows.

Below: The border from a printed curtain fabric is ideal for a straight pelmet.

Covered in a furnishing fabric to complement your curtains and shaped to suit the style of your décor, a pelmet never fails to add a distinctive touch to a room.

The material traditionally used to stiffen fabric pelmets is buckram interfacing, a woven fabric which has been treated to become rigid. More modern alternatives include self-adhesive non-woven materials, such as Rufflette Pelmform. This has a peel-off backing paper printed with several different pelmet silhouettes to follow when cutting out and with a grid to simplify drawing out your own design. One type of Pelmform is velour-backed thus eliminating the need for lining. These stiffenings can be bought by the metre from furnishing fabric departments.

Almost any furnishing fabric, except very open weaves and sheers, can be used to cover the pelmet. If using buckram, back your chosen fabric with bump interlining or an iron-on interfacing for a smooth finish.

Attach your pelmet to the pelmet board with touch-and-close fastener – Sew 'n' stick Velcro is ideal. This makes adding decorative braid (traditionally applied to cover tackheads) purely a matter of choice.

Hanging a pelmet

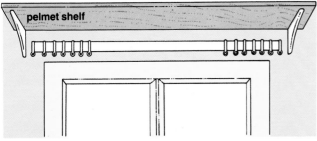
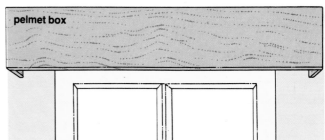

Pelmets must be attached to a firm support, called a pelmet board.

A pelmet shelf – simply a wooden shelf about 10-15cm/4-6in deep permanently attached to the wall just above the curtain track and/or architrave – is adequate for most windows. It should extend about 6cm/2½in beyond each end of the track.

A pelmet box, which also has narrow front and side box-style sections, gives the extra rigidity which may be needed for wide or particularly deep pelmets.

On deeply recessed windows, the pelmet board can be just a simple flat panel fixed across the top of the window area, level with the wall. When putting up a new pelmet shelf or box, bear in mind that, as the top edge of the pelmet will lie level with the top edge of the pelmet board, this will form the top edge of the window area. Consider therefore, the height and depth of the pelmet in relation to the window and to the height of the ceiling, not forgetting that the pelmet must be low enough to cover curtain track, before positioning a pelmet board.

Once screwed to the wall, a pelmet board becomes a permanent fixture which will probably outlast several pelmets. A pelmet, on the other hand, should be easy to remove for cleaning, while decorating, or to be replaced by a new one. Touch-and-close fastener, such as Velcro, is therefore ideal for attaching it. Tack or glue the hooked half of the Velcro all along the top edge of the front and sides (or returns) of the pelmet board (or use the self-adhesive half of Sew 'n' stick Velcro) and stitch the other half to the pelmet lining while making up.

Choosing fabric and a shape for your pelmet

Whatever the room scheme, pelmets can be pretty and decorative, classic and elegant, or stylishly simple to complement it. Choose a firmly-woven fabric to match, contrast or co-ordinate with your curtains and echo the style of the fabric design in the pelmet shape you choose – a prettily scalloped shape, for example, would not suit a sharp geometric print.

You can, if using Pelmform, follow one of the shapes printed on the backing paper. Alternatively, draw up your own design, perhaps copying or adapting one of the styles illustrated here, devising your own shape, opting for a simple rectangle, or following the outlines of motifs printed on the fabric.

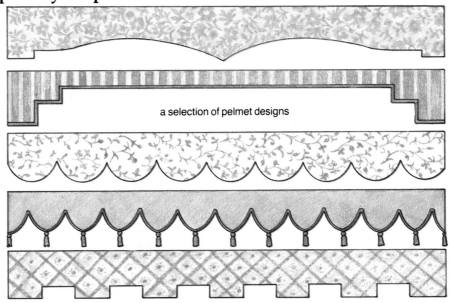

a selection of pelmet designs

Making a fabric pelmet

Put up a pelmet board, selecting the most suitable method of making a pelmet. This varies according to the type of stiffening used.

You will need

Buckram or Pelmform for stiffening
Fabric to match or contrast with curtains
Lining fabric (unless using one-sided Pelmform)
Interlining such as bump (if using buckram)
Paper to make a template (wallpaper is useful because of its length)
Velcro fastening
Decorative braid and fabric adhesive if desired

Making a template

Measure the length of the pelmet board including returns (short side ends) and cut a straight strip of paper to this length and slightly deeper than the widest section of your chosen pelmet shape. Fold the paper in half crosswise and mark the central point with a crease, and also crease the position of the corners.

Open out the paper and draw the intended shape on it, working from the centre out to the corner folds, and measuring accurately to make sure that any repeated shapes are of equal size and spacing. The returns can be shaped or left plain as desired. Fold the paper in half again and cut the shape from the doubled paper to ensure both sides are the same. Trim the top edge if necessary to make the template the exact size and shape of your finished pelmet, and check its proportions against your windows, adjusting if necessary.

Cutting out

Using the template, cut out the pelmet shape from buckram or Pelmform. Both are available in narrow widths so that the length can be cut from one piece without

Making up with traditional buckram

The traditional method of making a buckram pelmet involves a lot of hand sewing which takes time but gives a very professional finish. If your machine has a zip or piping foot, use the quick method.
Traditional method Place bump interlining centrally on the wrong side of the main fabric, and lock stitch together at intervals (see page 47). Place the buckram centrally on top of the bump interlining. Clipping into the border of fabric around curves or at corners, and trimming away excess where necessary, fold the fabric edges on to the wrong side of the buckram.

If using iron-on buckram, which is glue-impregnated, dampen the edges and stick down the fabric turnings by ironing in place. Otherwise slipstitch the edges of the fabric to the buckram.
Turn in the raw edges of the lining to make it 5mm/¼in smaller all round than the pelmet, clipping and trimming as necessary; press. Stitch the soft half of a strip of Velcro to right side along top edge of lining. Position the lining centrally on the wrong side of the buckram and slipstitch all round to hold.
Quick method Lock interlining to the fabric as above (or use iron-on

quick method

buckram

stitching holding
Velcro to lining

interfacing). Smoothing out the fabric, tack buckram to interlined side. Stitch the soft half of the Velcro 4cm/1½in down from the top edge of the lining strip. Lay fabric and lining right sides together and tack securely all round edge of

Making up with self-adhesive stiffening

Backings such as Rufflette Pelmform may cost a little more than buckram but are available in different widths for economy and are extremely simple to use. They are particularly helpful if you wish to follow one of the ready printed designs to shape the pelmet edge. Choose between velour backed or double-sided adhesive styles.
Ready-backed type The back of this type of stiffening is coated in a velour-style finish to make lining unnecessary and the front is self-adhesive.
Using your template, cut out the pelmet shape you require. If

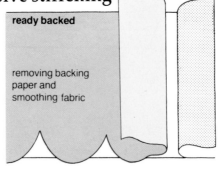

ready backed

removing backing
paper and
smoothing fabric

following one of the printed outlines for the lower edge, place the centre of your template either in the exact centre of a scallop or at the point between two shapes.
Ease the backing paper away from

the centre of the pelmet shape and cut it across the width. Peel back the paper for a little way on either side of the cut and place the wrong side of your fabric centrally on the exposed area of adhesive. Continue peeling back the paper while smoothing the fabric onto the stiffening adhesive, working from centre outwards so fabric remains absolutely smooth and wrinkle-free.
Press the backing and fabric firmly together and then, using sharp scissors, trim the fabric edges in line with the backing. Stick or tack the coarser hooked side of Velcro to the

Right: Trimming emphasizes the unusual shaping of a plain fabric pelmet.

much wastage; joins are not advisable as they tend to create ridges and will reduce the rigidity of the pelmet.

If using buckram, cut out the same shape in bump, for interlining, butting the edges together and herringbone stitching to join widths. Cut out fabric and lining 2.5cm/1in larger all round than the template. Plain fabrics can sometimes be cut along the length to avoid joins but if your fabric has a one-way design or a definite nap, you may need to join widths with narrow flat seams to make up a strip large enough for the pelmet. To avoid a centre seam, join extra fabric to either side of a central panel. Press seams open.

buckram. Trim lining level with top edge of buckram.

Using a zipper or piping foot, machine stitch as close to the edge of the buckram as possible around sides and lower edge.

Trim the seam to 1.5cm/⅝in, clip into curves and angles and across corners, then turn right side out. Press well, creasing the edges and smoothing the seam towards the lining side rather than the right side.

Press the top edge of fabric over the lining, turn in the raw edge, trimming if necessary, and slipstitch to lining just above the Velcro strip.

pelmet board. The velour backing clings to this without needing the other half of Velcro. Although not generally necessary except as a decorative effect, or on fabrics that have a marked tendency to fray, it may be advisable to stick a decorative braid around the cut edges for a neater finish.

Double-sided adhesive type This does need lining but it gives a more professional finish.

Cut the lining and the stiffening to the finished shape. Stitch the soft half of Velcro along the top edge on the lining, 2.5cm/1in down. Stick the main fabric onto right side

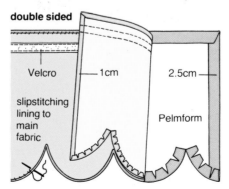

of stiffening as above but leaving a 2.5cm/1in turning all round. Clip into the turning around curves and into angles.

Press a 1cm/½in turning to the wrong side all round lining piece.

Removing the backing paper as you work, fold the fabric edges onto the wrong side of the pelmet, smoothing down so that they adhere.

Working from the centre outwards, stick wrong side of lining to wrong side of pelmet, overlapping the fabric edges. Slipstitch round lining to secure in place.

Add any braid trimmings required, slipstitching in place.

Attach hooked half of Velcro to pelmet board to correspond with soft half and press pelmet in place to hang. Do not use Pelmform for silk fabrics.

Curtain valances to frame your windows

Elegant and formal or frilly and charming, a curtain valance adds a decorative feature to your window. The wide choice of easy-to-make styles can be fitted on a pole, shelf or curtain track and only the hand-pleated headings require much sewing skill.

Curtain valances are often confused with pelmets, but in fact a pelmet is a rigid fitting, either in wood or fabric-covered wood, whereas a valance is a soft fabric drape. Both are used to disguise the tops of curtains and the curtain track, as well as enhancing the proportions of the window or adding a decorative feature.

The curtain valances shown here can be hung on tracks, poles, rods or a simple shelf-style fitting, above an existing curtain.

Style and proportion

If possible, hang the curtains before finally deciding on the style and depth of the valance.

The style will depend on the fabric the curtains are made from and on the way the room is furnished. A gathered valance made from a fresh, printed cotton will give a pretty, country look, while a valance of regular or grouped pleats will provide a more formal touch for heavier fabrics. A draped valance can be used for either look depending on the lightness of the fabric and on the surrounding furnishings.

The depth of the valance depends on the proportions of the window and personal taste. It can be used to improve the look of a window. For example, a deep valance will lower a tall narrow window, or help to obscure an unsightly view, while a shorter valance allows in the maximum of light through a small or shaded window.

There are no hard and fast rules that set the size of valance in relation to the curtain. If you start with the valance being one sixth of the curtain drop, this gives a point from which to

Left: Bound edges and a fabric-covered batten add style to a gathered valance.

work. Bear in mind that the valance must cover the track on which it is hung, the curtain track and the heading of the curtains.

Valance fittings

There are four main methods for fitting curtain valances: rod or tube, wooden pole, shelf or track.

Rod or tube fitting If the valance is hanging within a recess, or if the side view is not critical, it can be made with a simple cased heading and threaded on to a narrow rod, tube or curtain wire, fixed with brackets or hooks at each end.

Wooden curtain pole fitting The valance can be hung from the rings of a wooden curtain pole with decorative ends and brackets. The pole should be approximately 12cm/5in longer than the curtain track and project far enough from the wall to allow for the curtains. The actual measurement of this projection will be determined by the depth of the brackets used.

Curtain track fittings A simple curtain track is suitable for a valance if it is fitted with extended brackets to clear the curtains; alternatively fittings are available to clip the valance track straight on to the curtain track brackets.

The valance track must extend forward from the wall at least 4cm/1½in in front of the curtain track so that it does not interrupt the free movement of the curtains.

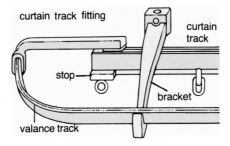

It is not practical to fix valance track above decorative curtain poles that extend away from the wall.

If both curtain and valance are to hang within a window recess, the valance track is the same width as the curtain track. Otherwise it should be longer and of the pliable type so that the ends can be bent back towards the wall to form sides or returns.

The valance is fitted to the track in the same way as a curtain, using curtain tape and hooks.

Shelf fittings If you cannot find a suitable track, pole or rod, fix a simple shelf supported by angle iron brackets above the curtain track. It should be 12cm/4¾in longer than the curtain track (unless in a recess) and protrude from the wall for 4cm/1½in more. Either attach the valance to the front and side edges of the shelf with upholstery tacks, gluing a decorative braid on top to hide the tack heads, or screw eyes round the shelf and attach the valance on to these with curtain hooks. The latter method allows the valance to be taken down for washing.

Measuring up

To find the depth most suitable for your valance, measure one sixth of the curtain drop and cut a strip of paper to this depth and as wide as your curtains. Carefully pin the paper to the top of the curtains in the correct position covering both tracks. Stand well back from the window and check the proportion of the valance in relation to the length of the curtains.

If it looks too deep, unpin the paper and trim off some of the depth. Repin and check again, repeating until you find the correct depth.

If the paper valance looks too shallow, make a new paper pattern with plenty of depth, and trim off until the correct proportion is reached. Remember that ultimately this is a matter of personal taste.

The depth of the fabric needed will be the paper pattern depth plus 2cm/¾in for the lower seam allowance, and a top seam allowance which varies according to the type of heading. The width of the fabric required depends on the type of heading used and fullness required.

If you have to join fabric strips to make up the width, join with 1.5cm/⅝in flat seams, neaten and press.

Making a valance with a taped heading

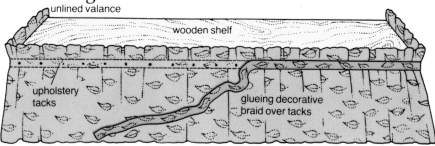

This style of valance is made as if it were a very short curtain (see pages 26-28 and 37-39). Choose the appropriate curtain tape to give a gathered, pencil pleated or triple pleated heading. Position the tape so that the valance will completely cover the track but still clear the ceiling. A standard gathering tape can be positioned 2cm/1in down from the top edge so that it creates a small upstanding frill along the top.

The valance can be made with just a single thickness of fabric like an unlined curtain or it can be given more body with an iron-on interfacing, in which case it should be lined for a neat finish. A valance with a triple-pleated heading particularly benefits from being interlined and lined.

The depth of fabric required will be as described plus a top seam allowance

of 4cm/1½in. The width will depend on the manufacturer's recommendation for the type of heading tape used.

An unlined valance

Measure up, cut out and join the fabric. Neaten the side and lower edges as for cased heading valances. Turn in the seam allowance along the top edge and pin the curtain tape into position to

cover the raw edge. Turn in the raw ends of the tape – but not the pulling up cords – and tack and stitch it in place.

Pull up the cords until the valance is the correct width and tie the ends to secure. Even out the pleats or gathers, insert curtain hooks and hang the valance in the same way as a curtain.

If you are using a wooden shelf fitment, line up the curtain tape

Making a valance with a hand-pleated heading

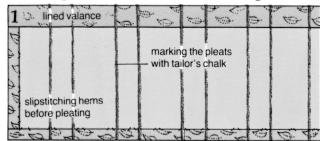

A pleated valance looks best if made with a stiffened fabric – interfaced and lined as the interlined valance with heading tape.

With a strip of paper, work out the size and type of pleat that will suit your valance and fit evenly into its length. Cut a piece of fabric of

sufficient depth and width (join pieces if necessary) to make the valance. Three times the finished width required, plus seam allowances, will be sufficient for continuous knife or box pleats. Allow 4cm/1½in for the top seam allowance.

Make up the valance in the same way as the lined version with curtain tape but, after folding over top seam allowance, do not add tape.

1 Following the pleat size from your experimental paper strip, mark out the valance into even divisions

Making a valance with cased heading

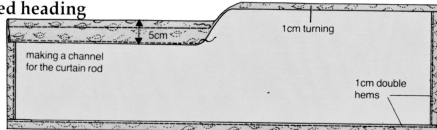

This is the easiest valance to make and hang as the supporting rod, tube or wire is simply threaded through the cased heading.

Measure the depth as described and add 6cm/2½in top seam allowance to enclose a rod up to 2cm in diameter between two rows of stitching.

For the width of fabric required allow one and a half to two times the length of the rod or pole.

Cut out your fabric to the required measurements, joining widths if necessary with 1.5cm/⅝in flat seam or French seam.

1 Turn a double hem (5mm/¼in and then 1cm/½in) to the wrong side down each side edge and stitch. Turn a double hem (1cm/½in and 1cm/½in) along the lower edge and stitch. (Alternatively, trim off lower seam allowance and bind edge with a contrasting binding.)

2 On the top edge, turn the seam allowance to the wrong side, then turn in the raw edge by 1cm/½in and stitch. Make another row of stitching 4cm/1½in above this one to form a channel through which the rod is threaded.

Press well and add any trimmings

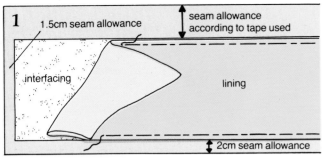

1 1.5cm seam allowance | seam allowance according to tape used | interfacing | lining | 2cm seam allowance

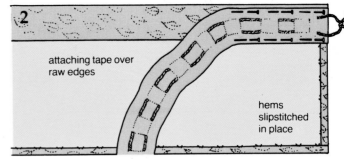

2 attaching tape over raw edges | hems slipstitched in place

with the facing edges of the shelf and attach the valance with upholstery tacks. Cover the tack heads with a decorative braid or a fabric-covered batten glued in place.

A lined valance

An interfacing such as iron-on Vilene can be added to give your fabric more body and a crisper look. There are several weights available – select the weight that, together with your fabric, will give the desired thickness.

A lining is necessary to give a neat finish and also protects the valance from sunlight.

Cut out the valance as for an unlined one, and cut the lining and interlining to the exact finished measurements without seam allowances. If necessary, join fabric widths and lining widths.

1 Position the interfacing to the wrong side of the fabric within the seamlines. Following the manufacturer's instructions for heat setting, dry iron the interfacing on to the fabric.

Lay lining on top of interfacing right side upwards and tack in place.

2 Turn in double hems along side and lower edges as for the cased valance, slipstitching down to the lining. Finish the top edge with heading tape.

using tailor's chalk on the wrong side. Fold and press the pleats, one by one, and tack in position.

2 Place a length of plain tape about 2.5cm/1in wide, on the wrong side of the valance to cover the raw edge (as with the heading tape) and sew in place.

You can hand sew the tape if you do not want the stitching lines to show on the right side, but you must be sure to stitch through all but the front layer of fabric in order to secure the pleats in place.

If necessary, neatly catchstitch the top edges of the pleats together on the right side.

Sew rings or hooks to the tape to attach the valance to its support.

before threading on to the rod. This method can be adapted for a simple gathered heading attached around a shelf fitting. Instead of adding the second row of stitching along the top edge, insert two rows of gathering stitches and pull up to the appropriate size. Nail it around the edge of the shelf and cover the nail heads with braid or a neatened bias strip of fabric. Turning in the ends of the braid to neaten, use fabric adhesive to glue in place.

Right: Rufflette Tridis tape gives regular triple pleating; hand-made pleats can be grouped or spaced out.

Draped valance with cascades

Complex swagged valances can be time consuming to make, but this simple draped valance with its cascades on each side gives an equally sumptuous effect for relatively little time and effort.

Choose a lining that is colour matched or use the same fabric for both valance and lining as it will tend to show. If you wish to use a sheer fabric for an unlined valance, omit any seam allowances and bind edges.

The valance is draped over a pair of wooden or metal brackets – such as the type used with curtain poles. Position the brackets just above and slightly outside each end of the curtain track.

Measuring up

To calculate the amount of fabric needed, use a tape measure (or a length of string) and drape it over the two brackets allowing it to drop into a gentle swag between them to hide the curtain track and headings. Allow it to hang down at either side of the window frame to measure the depth of cascade required.

Measure the total length of the tape or string (A–A) to give you the total width of fabric needed, adding 3cm/1¼in for seam allowances. Measure the drop of the swag between the two brackets (B–B) and also the distance in a straight line between the two brackets (C–C).

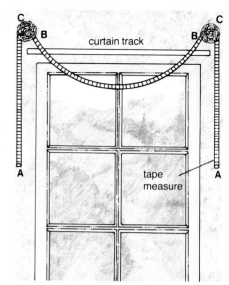

Making up the draped valance

Cut a piece of fabric the width from A to A plus 3cm/1¼in, joining widths if necessary, with a depth of 120cm/47¼in.

1 With tailor's chalk, mark the distance B–B centrally on one long side of the fabric. Draw diagonal lines to join B to A on each side and cut the fabric along these two lines. Now cut a piece of lining fabric to exactly the same size and shape. Tack the lining fabric and valance fabric together right sides facing. Sew the lining and valance fabric together all round, taking a 1.5cm/⅝in seam and leaving a 20cm/7in gap for turning through. Trim the seam to 1cm/½in and clip off each corner close to the stitching line. Turn to the right side and slipstitch the opening closed. Press.

On the lining side, mark the distance between the two C points centrally on the longest side.

2 Join points C and B with chalk lines, then sew a length of standard heading tape along each line. Knot the ends of the cord at the B edge, leaving them loose for pulling up on the C edge.

Pull up the cords in the heading tape to gather the fabric and then lay the gathers over the brackets. Adjust the cascades if necessary. If the fabric shows a tendency to slip, tie the ends of the heading tape cords around the brackets so that they don't show.

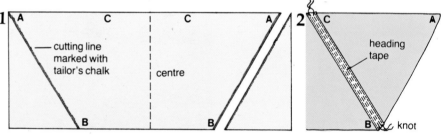

Right: The valance can be draped over brass curtain holders or wooden brackets.

Decorative curtain borders for a stylish finish

Add a decorative edging when making up new curtains or to highlight an old pair. Choose a style which suits the room – a frilled edge for a pretty finish, a piped edge for elegance or a bold contrast border or appliqué motif for a striking feature.

Below: Bear in mind the proportions of your curtains when choosing the width and position of a border and use bold colour contrasts for a dramatic effect.

Give curtains a designer style finish by adding a frill or piping to the edges or by applying a fabric border or appliqué motifs. These can easily be incorporated when making up new curtains, but the ideas can be adapted to brighten up an old pair if you unpick hems and sewn-in linings as necessary.

Cut out the curtain fabric and join widths if necessary, following instructions given on pages 26-27 and 42-44. For curtains with sewn-in linings, cut the lining to the *same width* as the curtain fabric.

Take 1.5cm/⅝in seam allowances throughout unless otherwise stated. Bear in mind the proportion of your curtains when deciding which edges are to be decorated. The most usual position is down the inner edge where the curtains meet, but outer and hem edges can be bordered too.

Making a gathered frill

A frill, whether applied to lined or unlined curtains, can be either a single or double thickness of fabric. Double thickness is generally preferable so that the right side of the fabric will show on both sides of the frill, but a single thickness is more suitable if the fabric is bulky.

To calculate the length of fabric for a frill, multiply the length of the edge to be frilled by one and a half to two times. The finished width of the frill should be about 10cm/4in for an average-sized curtain.

For a double-thickness frill cut fabric to the required length (joining strips if necessary), and to double the finished width of the frill plus 3cm/1¼in for seam allowances. Fold the fabric in half along its length, wrong sides facing, and run two rows of gathering threads along the raw edge of the frill, just inside the seam allowance and stitching through both layers of fabric. If you are using a machine, gather in sections no longer than 1m/1yd to make it easier to pull up the threads without breaking.

For a single-thickness frill cut fabric to the required length (joining strips if necessary), and to the width of the finished frill plus 3cm/1¼in for seam and hem allowance. Neaten one long edge with a double hem, 5mm and 1cm/ ¼in and ⅜in. Run two rows of gathering threads along the other long edge, within the seam allowance.

Applying the frill

Gathered frills can be applied to both lined and unlined curtains.
Unlined curtains Pull up the gathering threads until the frill fits between the top and bottom hem lines of the curtain fabric. With right sides and raw edges together, tack frill to curtain fabric. Sew frill in place with a 1.5cm/⅝in seam and zigzag raw edges together to neaten. Press frill out from curtain. This method is also used for curtains with detachable linings.
Lined curtains Pull up the gathering threads until the frill fits between the top and bottom hem lines of the curtain fabric. With right sides and raw edges together, tack the frill to the curtain fabric. Place the lining and curtain fabric right sides together, sandwiching the frill, and sew side seams with 1.5cm/⅝in seams. Trim the seam allowances and turn right side out so that the frill protrudes from the seam.

Complete curtains in the usual way.

Making fabric borders

A ready-made printed border is the easiest kind to apply. They are available in different widths and a wide variety of colours and designs to match or complement a particular range of wallpapers and fabrics.

You can make your own borders from furnishing fabrics to match or contrast with your curtains. Choose fabrics of similar weight as the curtains to ensure they hang well. Borders can be applied to the edges of both lined and unlined curtains. Decide which edges of the curtain are to be trimmed and the width of the border in proportion to the curtain.

Making the border strips

Cut strips of fabric the length of each border plus 2cm/1in seam allowances all round. Try to cut each section in one continuous strip – if you join strips match the pattern, if there is one, as necessary.

With tailor's chalk, mark the finished side edges and the top and bottom hem foldlines on to the right side of each curtain.

Press the seam allowance to the wrong side on both long edges.

Applying the border

Tack the border to the right side of the curtain fabric, one edge close to the side chalk line. Turn under the short edges to lie along top and bottom hem lines.

If the borders continue around the bottom of the curtain, form a mitre at the corner where they join. Fold the ends at a 45° angle and press. Cut away the excess fabric, leaving a small seam allowance. Slipstitch the mitred edges together or, with right sides together, machine along foldline and open out.

Machine topstitch the borders on to the curtains, then make up the curtains in the usual way.

Making an appliqué border

For a really original touch, appliqué can be used to form a border around a curtain. The motifs can be applied to both lined or unlined curtains before making up. It is best to choose one or two simple motifs to repeat along the edge to form the border.

Making the appliqué motif

To check that the design is in proportion to the curtain, pin a paper pattern on to the curtain fabric to judge the size and position. When you are satisfied with the pattern make an accurate template of the motif. Position it on the right side of the curtain fabric and draw round the template as often as necessary until the appliqué has been accurately marked out.

Use the template to cut out the appliqué shapes from the border fabric. Choose a fabric which matches the weight of the curtain fabric if possible, but if a lightweight fabric is chosen back the motifs with iron-on Vilene.

Applying the motifs

Place each motif within its chalk outline and tack to the curtain. Use a close zigzag stitch to machine over the raw edges of each motif.
If you do not have a swing needle

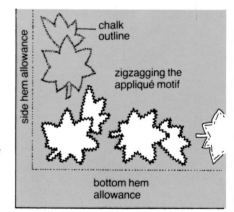

machine, sew round the raw edges with a close buttonhole stitch.
When the appliqué is complete, make up curtains in the usual way.

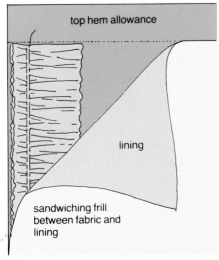

top hem allowance

lining

sandwiching frill
between fabric and
lining

*Right: A gathered curtain frill
emphasizes a pretty fresh cotton print.
Highlight a matching frill with piping
in an accent colour or choose a
contrasting fabric. Echo the frill on
tie-backs, cushions or a bedspread.*

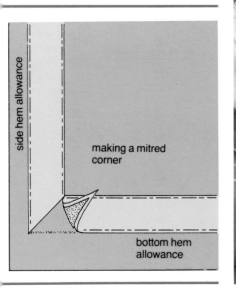

side hem allowance

making a mitred
corner

bottom hem
allowance

Making a piped edge

Piping down the inside and possibly even the outside edges of curtains provides a subtle accent of colour. The piping is inserted between two layers of fabric so this trimming is not suitable for unlined curtains or those with detachable linings.

Making the piping

Cut piping cord to the exact finished length of each edge to be piped. Cut bias strips of fabric wide enough to cover the cord plus 3cm/1¼in seam allowance. Join bias strips to 3cm/1¼in longer than edge to be piped. Wrap the fabric strips, right sides outwards, around the cord and tack the two layers together as close to the cord as possible. Using the zipper foot on your sewing machine, stitch close to the cord. Remove tacking. Alternatively, you can use purchased ready-made piping.

Applying the piping

Tack piping to the right side of the curtain fabric, raw edges together. Place the lining and curtain fabric right sides together, sandwiching the piping between. Tack through all layers close to the piping cord, then machine stitch with a zipper foot.

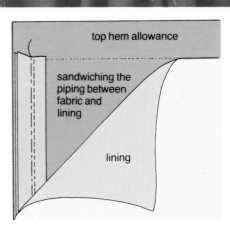

top hem allowance

sandwiching the
piping between
fabric and
lining

lining

Turn the curtain and lining through to the right side, so that the piping protrudes from the seamline. Make up curtains in the usual way.

Curtain tiebacks for a designer look

Tiebacks can be both pretty and practical. Choose a simple curved band or add piping, pleats or flounces for decoration. They make plain curtains more interesting, hold full ones back from a window or door or tie back the hangings round a four-poster bed.

They're only small, and often sadly forgotten, but curtain tiebacks are very useful and can give a new lease of life to a pair of dull or old curtains. A remnant of fabric is all that is needed – choose it to match the curtains, or to tone or contrast.

Make the tiebacks perfectly plain, or pipe them, add a ruffle, pleats or scallops; make them straight or gently curved.

As an alternative to using fabric, a length of chunky dressing gown cord makes a graceful, elegant tieback for full-length velvet curtains. Other ideas can come from furnishing braids, dress trims and ribbons.

You will need

Fabric Most light, closely woven furnishing fabrics are suitable. Don't try to use heavy brocades or velvet as they will not make up successfully – the fabric is too bulky. Both sides of the tieback can be of furnishing fabric, but if you haven't got enough, or the fabric is expensive or bulky, you can use a toning lining fabric for the backing.

Interfacing Use pelmet buckram or firm Vilene interfacing.

4 small curtain rings and two hooks for fixing to wall

Sewing thread

Paper for making patterns

Measuring up

To calculate where to place the tieback and how long and wide it should be, loop a tape measure around the curtain about two-thirds down from the top and arrange the curtain into the curve or folds you want. Note the measurement on the tape measure as this gives the length of the finished tieback. While the tape measure is still in place, make a small pencil mark on the wall to indicate the position for fixing the hook.

For sill-length curtains, the depth of the tieback should be no more than 10cm/4in, but for longer curtains it may be enlarged proportionally. Instructions given here are for 10cm/4in depth tiebacks. Seams throughout are 1.5cm/⅝in unless otherwise stated.

Right: This attractive square bay window is ideal for four separate curtains. The tiebacks hold them back during the day to allow in plenty of light.

Making a straight-edged tieback

This is very simple to make up and any of the variations shown overleaf can be added.

Cut a paper pattern to the length required × 10cm/4in deep. Pin the pattern to a double thickness of fabric and cut out (or cut out once in fabric and once in lining), allowing an extra 1.5cm/⅝in all round for seams.

Pin the pattern to a single thickness of interfacing and cut out without any seam allowance.

1

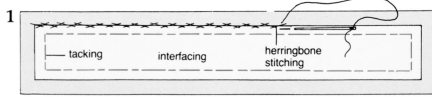

tacking   interfacing   herringbone stitching

2

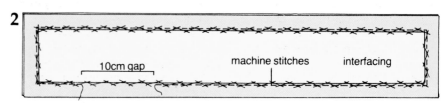

10cm gap   machine stitches   interfacing

1 Lay the interfacing centrally on the wrong side of one piece of fabric. Tack together. Herringbone stitch all round the edges of the interfacing to catch to fabric. Work the herringbone stitch from left to right, first taking a small stitch horizontally in the tieback fabric and then diagonally opposite and lower down on the interfacing. The stitches should not show on the right side of the tieback fabric.

2 Place the two tieback pieces right sides facing and tack together all round, leaving a 10cm/4in gap for turning through to the right side. Machine with the interfacing uppermost, being careful to sew close to, but not over, the edge of the interfacing.
Trim the seams and clip diagonally across the corners. Remove tacking. Turn through to right side and slipstitch the open edges together to close. Press.

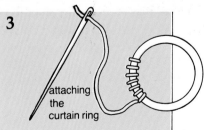

attaching the curtain ring

3 Sew a curtain ring to the middle of each short edge. Working on the wrong side of the fabric, overcast the ring just inside the edge so that most of the ring protrudes.

Making a shaped tieback

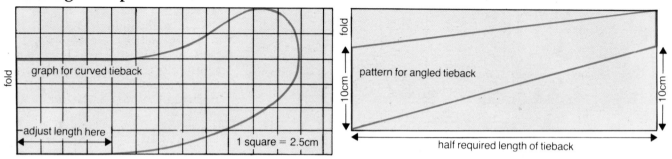

A **curved tieback** gives an elegant shape that echoes the graceful lines of a draped curtain.

Cut a piece of paper to the length of the tieback × 15cm/6in deep and fold in half widthways. Divide into 2.5cm/1in squares and scale up the diagram shown to draw in the curve.

Cut out the paper pattern, open out flat, and cut out twice in fabric, with an additional 1.5cm/⅝in all round for the seam allowance. Cut out once in interfacing.

Continue to make up as for the straight-edged tieback.

An **angled tieback** gives a streamlined shape that is easy to emphasise with trimmings.

Cut a piece of paper to the length of the tieback × 15cm/6in.

Fold the paper in half widthways and mark a point 10cm/4in up on each short side. Join points to diagonally opposite corners as shown to make the tieback shape. Make up as for a straight tieback.

Trimming tiebacks

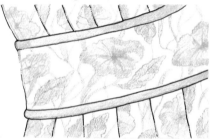

A plain tieback looks very smart but it also lends itself to additional trimmings that create a softer, crisper or more feminine look.

Piped edges Piping in the seam line emphasises shape and can provide a contrast colour. Either cover the piping cord with bias strips cut from the same fabric as the tieback or use purchased bias binding, 2.5cm/1in wide. Cover the cord and apply to the right side of one piece of the tieback, raw edges together. Continue making up the tieback as before, but sandwiching the piping between the two layers of fabric. Use a zipper foot to sew the seam, stitching as close to the piping as possible.

Left: Cut tieback patterns in paper and adjust their proportions to suit your curtains. These curved tiebacks were narrowed down to allow for the addition of a deep frill.

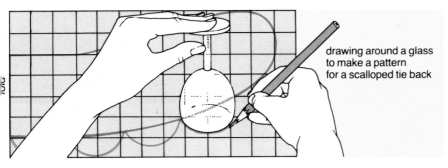

drawing around a glass to make a pattern for a scalloped tie back

A scalloped tieback can be made straight or curved.

Draw up a pattern for the basic shape of tieback you require but on deeper paper. Using a suitable size curve – an egg-cup or the rim of a small wine glass – draw a series of even-sized scallop shapes along the lower edge of the paper pattern. Start with a full scallop at the fold and, when you reach the end, adjust to finish with either a half or a complete scallop.

Cut out the paper pattern and open out flat. Cut out twice in fabric with an additional 1.5cm/⅝in all round for the seam allowance. Cut out once in interfacing without a seam allowance.

Continue to make up the tieback as before, sewing carefully around the scallop shapes and snipping into the curves – taking care not to snip the stitching – before turning through to the right side.

As an alternative, you can zigzag the edges of the scallops with a contrasting coloured sewing thread. Cut out the fabric as for the scalloped edge and attach the interfacing. Right sides facing, sew the two pieces together along the top and two side edges only. Turn to the right side and press.

On the scalloped edge, trim the seam allowance so that the fabric and interfacing edges match. Tack the two scalloped edges together around the edge of each scallop. Using a contrast coloured sewing thread and a close machine zigzag stitch, machine very carefully around the curve of each scallop, so that the zigzag stitch covers the raw edges of the fabric.

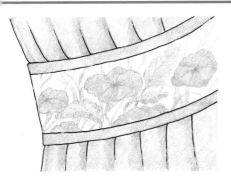

Bound edges Binding all round the edges gives the chance to introduce a contrast colour, or to pick up a plain colour from a patterned fabric. Again, you can use bias strips cut from the fabric or purchased bias binding. Cut out the fabric and interfacing to the shape you require, without any seam allowance.

Wrong sides facing, sandwich the interfacing between the two pieces of fabric, and tack together around the edges. Round off any corners slightly to make it easier to apply the binding. Attach bias strips or bias binding, slipstitching in place on the wrong side.

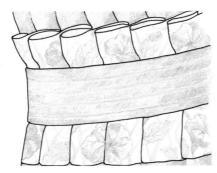

Pleated edges These are most suitable for straight-edged tiebacks. Cut from fabric two pleating strip pieces 11cm/4½in wide × three times the length of the tieback plus 3cm/1¼in.

Right sides facing, fold each pleating strip in half lengthways and sew across each short end. Turn right side out and press. Press in knife pleats, 1.5cm/⅝in wide, all facing in the same direction, along the total length of each pleating strip.

Lay the two pleated strips, one along either long edge, on the right side of one tieback piece, raw edges matching and 1.5cm/⅝in in from the short edge at each end. Adjust pleat depth slightly if the length is not quite accurate. Tack in place. Continue to make up as for the straight-edged tieback.

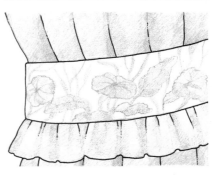

Frilled edges Open the pattern flat, and cut two pieces in fabric with an extra 1.5cm/⅝in seam allowance all round. Measure along the bottom edge of the tieback and cut enough 7.5cm/3in wide pieces of fabric to give a frill piece double this measurement when they are joined. Turn a double hem (5mm/¼in and then 1cm/½in) to the wrong side along one long edge of the frill piece and along the two short edges. Sew two lines of gathering threads along the remaining raw edge, 1cm/½in and 1.5cm/⅝in from the edge. Place the frill on one tieback piece, right sides facing and with raw edges together. Pin each end of the frill 1.5cm/⅝in in from the side edges of the tieback, and pull up the gathering threads until the frill, when evenly gathered, fits along the edge of the tieback. Tack in place. Continue to make up the tieback as for the straight version, being careful not to catch the free ends of the frill in the side seams.

Practical café curtains

These curtains were traditionally used in French cafés to cover the lower half of the window. They are easy and economical to make in a variety of styles – simply gather the top with a taped heading or cut a scalloped edge which can be plain or pleated.

Traditional café curtains cover only the lower half of a window, giving privacy without too much loss of light. They hang from brass or wooden poles, known as café rods, and because of their rather informal look they are most often used in kitchens and bathrooms. They can be unlined to give maximum light but, as with any curtain, a lining does protect the fabric and give added insulation.

Several variations on the traditional single curtain across the lower part of the window are shown below right. You can add a curtain valance at the top of the window. You can combine a single lower curtain with a pair of short upper curtains which can be opened to let in daylight and drawn together at night. Alternatively both lower and upper curtains can be pairs.

Café curtains often have a simple gathered top, but perhaps the most distinctive style is the scalloped top, either plain or with triple pleating between the scallops. This chapter concentrates on how to make up this highly decorative variation.

For either style, fix the support brackets and place the pole in position so that the exact drop of the curtain can be measured before cutting out.

The pole for the lower curtain is positioned at least halfway up the window, coinciding with a window bar if there is one at about the required level. The finished curtain should be sill length.

For a valance or top curtains, the pole can be fixed either just above the window frame or within the recess. The top curtains should overlap the lower curtain by about 10cm/4in.

Choosing fabrics

The plain scalloped style of café curtain should be made in a furnishing fabric with a reasonable amount of body or it will not hang well. The other styles, however, do not neces-

Right: Disguise an uninspiring view with a pretty café curtain made with a cased heading and a frilled hem.

sarily need to be made in curtaining at all – choose a printed dress cotton, fresh gingham, cotton lace or a sheer fabric such as voile to complement the style of the room.

Simple gathered café curtain

This can be made in the same way as ordinary curtains with a simple cased heading and threaded on to a narrow rod or a curtain wire. (See pages 26-27 and 33 for making up instructions.) Alternatively, use a curtain heading tape to gather or pleat the top, insert hooks and hang it from the rings of a wooden or brass curtain pole. (See pages 37-39 and 42-44 for lined and unlined versions.)

Scalloped café curtain

An attractive scalloped edge shows to full advantage on a café curtain. It can also be a very economical use of fabric as the curtain is virtually flat – at the most slightly undulating – rather than gathered. If a fuller look is required, pleats can be formed between each scallop.

Curtain rings or hooks are sewn on to the strips between scallops to hang the curtain. Alternatively, crocodile clips are available which hook into the curtain rings and clip to the top of the curtain.

You will need to make a paper pattern for the scalloped edge before cutting out the curtain. The scallop size given overleaf will suit most average windows but it can be adjusted for a particularly large or small curtain. If you want to line the curtain, cut both fabric and lining and join using the sewn-in lining method (see page 42). Tack the top edge of the lining level with the foldline of the curtain top before sewing the scalloped top.

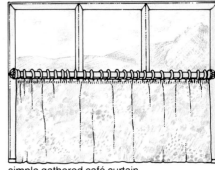

simple gathered café curtain

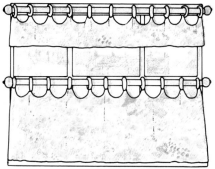

café curtain with valance

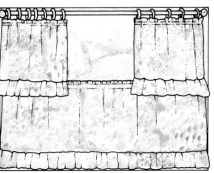

café curtain with pair of upper curtains

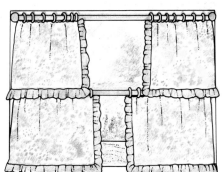

both upper and lower curtains in pairs

Making a plain scalloped curtain

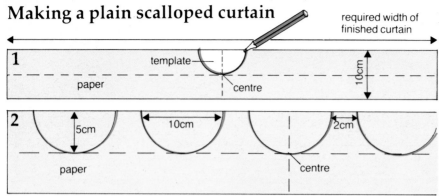

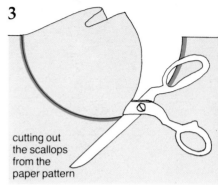

cutting out the scallops from the paper pattern

The scalloped top gives style to a flat curtain. Because there is no fullness, choose a furnishing fabric with a fair amount of body rather than a soft or sheer material.

Cutting the pattern An exact semi-circle makes a scallop that is visually pleasing. Use a pair of compasses or a suitable size saucer to draw a circle 10cm/4in in diameter on to thin card. Cut out the circle then cut it across the diameter to make a semi-circular template. Measure the width of the window fairly generously as the curtain will be flat but not absolutely taut. Cut a strip of paper to the required width of

the finished curtain by 10cm/4in deep. Fold in half along the length and width to find the centre.
1 Place the template in the centre of the strip as shown – between the top edge and the centre line – and draw round it to mark the centre scallop.
2 Leaving a 2cm/1in space between each one, and working from the centre to one edge, lightly pencil in further scallops. Ideally, the last scallop will finish about 2cm/1in from the edge but, if you end up with a half scallop, either increase the width of the paper pattern (which will give your curtain a

softer less flat effect) or adjust the spacing between scallops and redraw the pattern. Repeat from the centre to the other end.
To work out the number of scallops and the spacing between them mathematically, take 2cm/1in (the ideal for the space) from the finished curtain width (to allow for a space at both ends) then divide this measurement by 12cm/5in (ie the size of one scallop plus one space). This will give you the number of scallops that will fit the width. If it is not a whole number, adjust the space between scallops until it is.

Making a pleated scalloped curtain

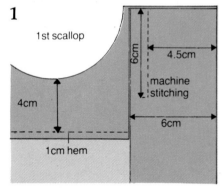

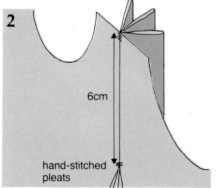

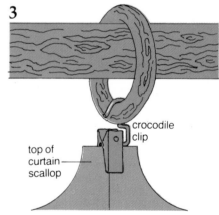

With this style a triple pleat is formed between each scallop to give the curtain more fullness.
Cutting the pattern Work out the number of scallops to fit across the width either by making a rough paper pattern or by calculating mathematically as for the plain scalloped curtain.
Having worked out the number of scallops required, make up a new paper pattern, leaving 12cm/5in between each scallop for the pleats. Although you will increase the fabric width you still have the same number of scallops as for the plain scalloped curtain.

Cutting out and making up Use the paper pattern to cut out the width of the curtain fabric, adding hem and seam allowances and joining widths if necessary, as for the plain version.
1 To form the pleats, fold the fabric between each scallop in half and, starting 4.5cm/2in from the fold, stitch down for about 6cm/2in from the top edge.
2 Make two folds within this pleat to form a triple pleat and tack in place.
Neatly hand stitch the pleats at the front at a point 6cm/2in from the top edge and at the back on the top edge to hold in place. Remove tacks.

Complete the hem along the lower edge as for the plain scalloped curtain.
3 Stitch a curtain ring or hook to the corners of each space between scallops or behind each set of pleats, depending on how much support your fabric needs. Alternatively, hang the curtain with crocodile clips which do not require stitching.

Right: A pleated scalloped curtain is bright and practical for the recess of a kitchen window. With an all-over print, the fabric can be used horizontally and cut in one piece.

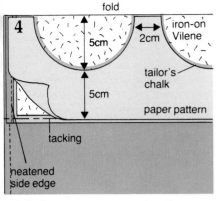
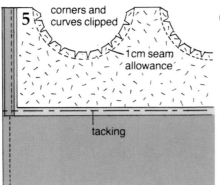
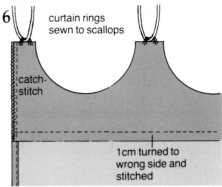

With these measurements, draw scallops along the whole strip.
3 When the paper pattern is completely drawn up, cut away the scallops.
Cutting out and making up Cut the curtain to the pattern width plus 3cm/1¼in seam allowances. If more than one width of fabric is needed allow 1cm/½in seam allowances, join selvedges and press seams open. Cut to the finished length plus a 5cm/2in bottom hem allowance and 10cm/4in for the top turning.
Neaten side edges by turning in 5mm/¼in and 1cm/½in and stitch.

Along the top edge of curtain, turn 10cm/4in of fabric to the right side and tack down. Cut a strip of iron-on Vilene 2cm/1in less than the curtain width and 9cm/3½in deep and iron on to the turned-over flap next to the fold and within the side seams.
4 Place the paper pattern on the flap with the straight edge of the scallops to the fold and draw round the scallop shapes with tailor's chalk. Remove pattern and machine stitch round each scallop following chalk lines.
5 Leaving 1cm/½in seam allowances, cut away each scallop.

Clip across corners and into seam allowances around each curve, remove tacks and turn flap to the wrong side of curtain, carefully turning out each scallop.
6 Turn 1cm/½in to the wrong side along bottom edge of flap and stitch. Catchstitch side edges together.
Sew a curtain pole ring centrally on the wrong side of each space between scallops. Complete the curtain by turning up and stitching the lower hem.

Shower curtains – meet splash with dash

*Keep splashes in check with a practical shower curtain.
Choose a stylishly simple version or
combine it with a fabric or towelling curtain for an
elegant and luxurious effect. Eyelets
and rings make hanging the curtain quick and simple.*

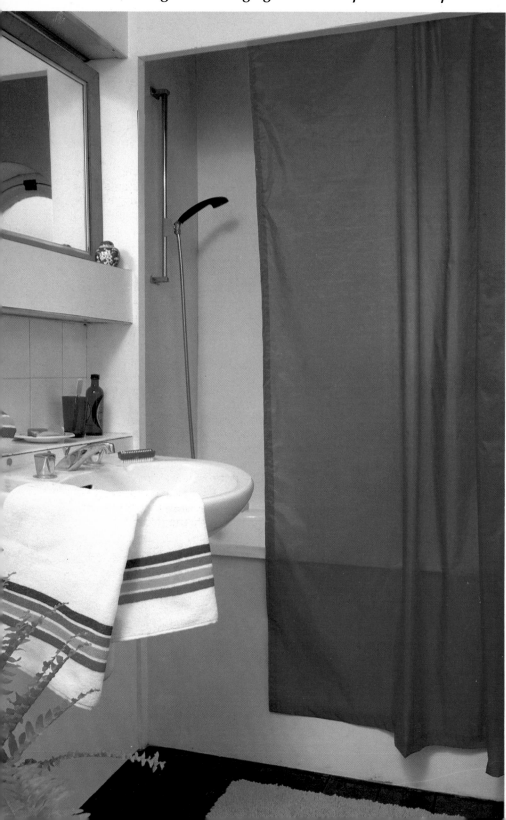

A curtain provides an inexpensive but effective method of keeping the splashes in check while having a shower. The shower curtain must have a waterproof surface and be long enough to tuck inside the bath or shower tray so that splashes of water are diverted by the curtain down the plug hole.

Shower curtains usually hang from a simple rail – you can buy shower rails from chain and hardware stores. There are expanding rails with suction ends which don't need to be screwed into the wall or through tiles and flexible rails which can be angled to fit around two or three sides of the shower.

The shower curtain is attached by means of large plastic rings which you simply thread on to the shower rail and clip together through eyelet holes made along the top edge of the shower curtain.

Inserting eyelets is very simple. You will need a large size of eyelet – 1cm/½in diameter – and a pair of eyelet pliers, or a kit which includes eyelets and a small hammer to insert them. The kit is much cheaper than the eyelet pliers.

You can of course hang the curtain by attaching a synthetic curtain heading tape and hooking this with curtain hooks on to the shower rail rings.

A basic shower curtain is made from a single unlined thickness of water-re-pellent rot-proof fabric, but to give your bathroom a more luxurious look, add an outer curtain that hangs over the outside of the bath. This can be made from normal curtaining fabric which, as it is protected by the inner curtain, can be trimmed and frilled to suit bathroom furnishings. The fabric side of the curtain must be completely detachable from the plastic or nylon side for laundering, so both plastic and fabric are made up as single thickness curtains and just joined together by sharing the same hooks on the rail. If your shower curtain hooks/rings will not take the bulk of two curtains or if you wish to gather the fabric curtain, use the curtain tape method described on pages 26-28 and insert a split ring to correspond with each eyelet on the ungathered plastic curtain.

Left: Waterproof rip-stop nylon, ideal for shower curtains, is available in strong, stylish colours.

Measuring up

Ready-made shower curtains are designed to fit along an average sized bath or around a shower and are about 180cm/70in square. This is a good standard size but, of course, not everyone's circumstances are standard. It is important that the curtain is of adequate size for the bath or shower, so measure up carefully before buying the fabric.

Shower curtains do not need to be gathered when pulled around the shower as gathering bunches up the curtain, trapping moisture and preventing the fabric drying off effectively. The outer curtain should not get wet so it can be gathered for a more draped effect.

The width Measure the curtain rail for the width of your shower curtain. The waterproof curtain should not be more than 1¼ times the measurement of the rail, but a perfectly flat shower curtain is quite adequate. Add 3cm/1¼in to each side for double side hems. Unless you are making a narrow shower curtain for a built-in shower unit, you will find that the fabrics generally available are not wide enough to make a shower curtain from a single width. Add 3cm/1¼in for each join in the fabric width.

The length Measure from the shower rail down to a point at least 20cm/8in inside the bath or almost to the floor in the shower tray. Add 6cm/2½in for a bottom double hem and 6cm/2½in for the top double hem to take the eyelets.

Choosing the fabric

The fabric for an unlined shower curtain, or for the shower side of a lined curtain, must be waterproof and unlikely to rot. Various synthetic materials such as 100% nylon, 100% pvc and 100% vinyl are available, usually in 130cm/51in widths, in patterned or plain colours. Rip-stop nylon, available from kite and sail shops, is also suitable and comes in a better range of bright colours.

Do not use pins on the fabric if they are likely to leave permanent holes. Hold the layers together with paper clips and use a wedge-pointed needle in the sewing machine.

These synthetic fabrics are not machine washable and should be wiped down with a soft cloth and non-abrasive cleaner.

Once a shower curtain is wet from use, it must be left as flat as possible to dry off. If it is drawn back and bunched up when wet, mildew can easily form and this is almost impossible to remove.

For a lined shower curtain, the fabric facing out into the bathroom does not need to be waterproof and can be chosen to co-ordinate with wallpaper, window curtains or other furnishings.

Towelling (but not the stretch variety) is an excellent choice, as it absorbs moisture but dries out quickly. The same colour towelling can be used for accessories such as bathrobes, towels and bath mat to give a co-ordinated effect which is essential in a small bathroom.

If you are using towelling, add at least 10% to your measurements and pre-wash the towelling before making up, to allow for its natural shrinkage.

A basic shower curtain

In the instructions below the 'right' side of the shower curtain is that which faces into the bathroom; the 'wrong' side faces into the bath or shower.

You will need
Waterproof fabric
Nylon or polyester thread
Eyelet kit or eyelet and pliers
Chinagraph pencil
Rail and rings

Cutting out and making up
Measure up as above and cut out including seam and hem allowances. Join widths if necessary with French seams (see page 27). If it is necessary to join widths of fabric the joins should be evenly spaced for the best visual effect. For example, if you are joining two pieces, join the two full widths and then cut off any excess from both sides so that the join is in the exact centre of the curtain.

On both side edges of the curtain, turn a double hem (1.5cm/⅝in and 1.5cm/⅝in) to the wrong side. Machine stitch in place close to the fold.

On the top edge, turn 3cm/1¼in then 3cm/1¼in as a double hem to the wrong side and machine stitch close to the lower folded edge.

Positioning the eyelets
To position the eyelets along the top hem, mark the fabric evenly about every 15cm/6in along the width of the curtain and about 1cm/½in down from the top edge. A chinagraph pencil makes a clear mark on plastic fabric and can be removed later with a soapy cloth. Check that you have sufficient shower curtain rings for the number of marks. If you do not have enough and are unable to buy any more to match, adjust the spacing evenly to tally with the number of rings. Follow the instructions supplied with the eyelet pliers or kit to make the holes and insert the eyelets.

Hanging the curtain
Hang the shower curtain by threading the rings/hooks on to the rail and clipping them through the eyelets.

Turn a double hem, 3cm/1¼in and 3cm/1¼in, along the bottom edge to the wrong side, and machine stitch in place close to the fold.

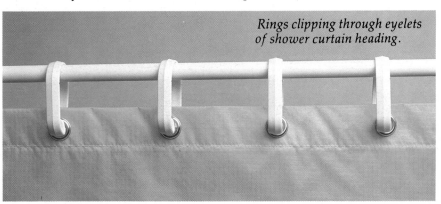

Rings clipping through eyelets of shower curtain heading.

Making a roller blind

Roller blinds are an attractive alternative to curtains, and need a fraction of the amount of fabric. They can be used as sunshades or to block out an ugly view and are simple to make from a kit. You can buy pre-stiffened blind fabric or stiffen a furnishing fabric yourself.

Blinds serve the same function as curtains, but they can also be used to cut out bright sunlight. When not in use they roll up out of the way, but their main advantage over curtains must be that they are so economical to make.

You need buy only the amount of fabric to cover the window area, plus a minimal amount top and bottom – there is no extra needed for pleats and gathers as in curtains and no need for lining fabric (although of course, lining fabric and fullness do make curtains better insulators.)

Roller blinds are useful at windows with radiators or furniture underneath them because they cover only the glass and need not hang below the sill. They look crisper and sharper than curtains and complement the clean lines of a modern room.

The blinds are quick and easy to put together. The straight bottom edge is the simplest to make, but the bottom of the blind can also be finished with decorative scallops or zigzag cuts. Alternative finishes are dealt with in the following chapter.

Right: A roller blind is ideal if you have furniture just beneath the window.

Decide whether you are going to hang your blind inside or outside the window recess – blinds are generally hung inside the recess.

1 Measure the width of the recess. If you are hanging the blind outside the recess, add 6cm/2¼in to allow for overlap. Buy a roller blind kit. They come in a range of standard sizes and, unless the width you need is a standard size, buy the next size up and cut the roller to fit. A 275cm/109in width is about the widest roller on sale.

2 Lay out the pieces of the roller kit to check you have everything you need. In most kits there is a wooden roller with a spring fitted at one end, an end cap and pin for the other end, two brackets, a wooden batten for the bottom of the blind,

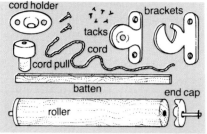

tacks, cord, a cord holder and a pull. Check the roller kit instructions for the positioning of each bracket. Normally two different brackets are supplied in each kit. The slotted bracket, which takes the spring end of the blind, usually goes on the left-hand side, unless you have chosen a non-reversible fabric. In this case, the roller can be fitted so that the fabric rolls over the front of

it with the right side of the fabric showing on the roller, rather than under the roller and down the back in the usual way.

If the fabric is non-reversible, fit the slotted bracket to the right-hand side of the recess for this alternative rolling up method.

If fixing your blind to the inside of the recess, position the brackets as close to the sides of the recess as

possible so that the maximum area is covered by the blind. Screw in the brackets tightly, making sure they are absolutely level.

If fixing it to the outside of the recess, the brackets should be at least 3cm/1¼in from the recess edge and at least 5cm/2in above it to prevent light from the window showing round the top and sides of the blind.

Cutting the roller to size

Measure the distance between the brackets with a steel or wooden rule and saw the roller to this width, making an allowance for the end cap, which you still have to fit. Fix the end cap and pin to the sawn end of the roller, following instructions supplied with the kit. The roller is now ready to take the fabric.

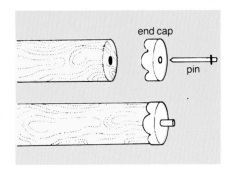

end cap

pin

Choosing and preparing the fabric

Use either commercially pre-stiffened fabric or a furnishing fabric, which you can stiffen at home.

Pre-stiffened roller blind fabric has been commercially treated to make it stiff, fray-resistant and, in some cases, spongeable and fade-resistant too. The fabric can be bought by the metre, in widths up to about 2m/2¼yd. Patterns without one-way designs can be used either vertically or horizontally to get the most economical use from the fabric.

Furnishing fabric as blind material
There are several do-it-yourself stiffening agents for roller blinds on the market. Choose a medium-weight fabric – too thin and it will not stiffen satisfactorily and will crease when rolled up – too thick and it will not roll up evenly. Many fabrics shrink slightly when stiffened, so treat the fabric before cutting it to size. Follow the instructions for stiffening provided with the product, testing a sample piece of fabric first to see if it is colour fast and can be stiffened.

Measuring up for the fabric
Measure the full width of your roller (excluding the protruding pin ends) and deduct 1cm/½in to arrive at the finished fabric width. Measure from the brackets down to the window sill, or to just below the sill for a blind hung outside the recess. Add 18cm/7in to allow for fixing round the roller and for a casing at the bottom for the wooden batten, to arrive at the fabric length. Pre-stiffened fabric will not fray when cut, and home-stiffened fabric should not do so either, so no

Cutting out and making up the blind

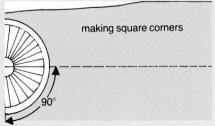

making square corners
90°

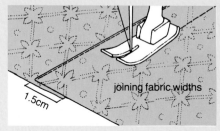

1.5cm
joining fabric widths

Work on a flat surface to prevent the fabric from creasing.
Cut the pre-stiffened or home-stiffened fabric to size using a sharp cutting knife or scalpel and a steel ruler or straight-edge tool as a cutting guide.
Square corners Each one must be an exact right angle, or the blind will always roll up unevenly and hang badly. Use a protractor or a carpenter's try square to mark exact 90° angles before cutting out.
Joining fabric widths The same method of joining widths can be used for both types of fabric. Overlap the two pieces of fabric by 1.5cm/⅝in and topstitch down both edges to secure.
Neatening fabric edges Pre-stiffened fabric is fray resistant and the

Fitting the batten

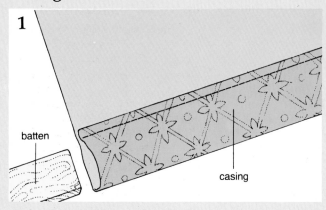

1
batten
casing

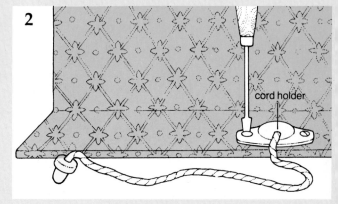

2
cord holder

Saw batten to 1cm/½in less than the width of the blind.
Turn a single hem about 4cm/1½in deep to wrong side along bottom edge. Check that the batten will slide easily into this space, and make the casing deeper if necessary.
1 Machine stitch close to the edge of the casing edge. On pre-stiffened fabric a zigzag stitch is preferable if your machine does this.
Slip the batten into the casing and sew up both ends with tiny overcast stitches.
If you do not have a sewing machine, cut the batten to size and fold the fabric to make the casing. Spread both sides of the batten with a fabric glue. Position it carefully inside the fold and weight down with heavy objects, such as books or kitchen weights, until the glue has dried.
You need to position the batten differently if the blind is to have a decorative bottom finish. (These are dealt with in the following chapter.)

To attach cord holder and cord
Push one end of cord through the hole in the cord holder, and knot behind it to secure.
2 Position cord holder at the centre of the batten casing, and screw in through the material. Generally the cord holder is fixed to the front of the blind, but you can screw it to the back to hide it from view.
Attach cord pull to end of cord.

allowance needs to be made for side and bottom hems.

If fabric has to be joined to make up the width of the blind, allow 1.5cm/⅝in seam allowance on each piece of fabric. Position the joins at equal intervals for the best appearance. **Patterned blinds** that have joins or are to hang close to one another, such as three blinds at a bay window, should be pattern matched (see page 44). When you measure up for the fabric make an allowance for the pattern repeats so that you can match them.

edges will not need neatening. Furnishing fabric should be fray-resistant once it has been stiffened, but if it does have a tendency to fray, zigzag the edges on a sewing machine. Never turn under a side hem, as this will give you an uneven thickness of fabric on the ends of the roller.

Right: Roller blinds team successfully with curtains; the two can be made up in complementary or matching fabrics.

Fixing the fabric to the roller

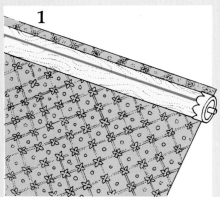
1

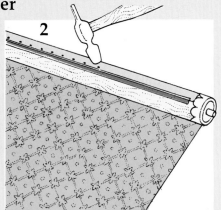
2

1 Lay the fabric flat, right-side upwards, and place the roller on the fabric at the top.

If you are making a blind in a non-reversible fabric and you have chosen the method of rolling the fabric over the roller rather than under it, you must lay the fabric *wrong* side upwards.

Lift the edge of the fabric over on to the roller, lining up with one of the horizontal marks on it. If your roller has no horizontal lines, clamp it in a carpenter's vice, or ask someone to

hold it very still for you, and mark a straight line at right angles to the ends along the length of the roller. Fix the edge of the fabric temporarily along this line with a length of sticky tape.

2 Hammer the small tacks provided with the kit through the edge of the fabric into the roller, spacing them evenly along it. Peel off the sticky tape.

(If you own or can borrow a staple gun, you'll find stapling the fabric to the roller is easier.)

Hanging the blind

Roll the fabric up tightly around the roller and fit it into the brackets. Pull the blind down to its full extent. You should now find that the tension is correct and when you give the cord a very gentle tug, the blind should roll up. If the tension is not correct, the blind will be sluggish and jerky as it rolls up or it may not roll up at all. Try again. Lift the extended blind out of the brackets and roll the fabric up round the roller. Put the blind back in the brackets and pull down again. Repeat until you get the correct tension, but be careful not to over-tension the blind or the spring may break.

79

Decorating roller blinds

Cut the lower edge of a blind into scallops, zigzags or a variety of wave shapes so that it remains a decorative feature of the room, even when pulled up. Add a braid trim to match your furnishings and finish the pull cord with a wooden acorn or a tassel.

Roller blinds are economical to make and practical to use but if you feel they leave windows looking rather bare when rolled up, add a decorative edging. Trim the lower edge of the blind into a dramatic wave shape, or cut a repeated shape such as scallops, inverted scallops or zigzags – choosing a style to suit the furnishings of the room.

Braid or lace trimmings can be added either to a straight edged blind or, if the fabric is likely to fray, to a cut, shaped edge.

On scalloped, zigzag and wave edged blinds, position the batten that straightens the lower edge of the blind above and well clear of any shaping or trimming. When the blind is pulled up, the shaping will still be visible, adding an attractive touch to the window.

There are two ways of making the batten casing and either can be used with any style of decorative edging given here.

The tuck method of making a blind casing leaves no surface stitching showing but is only suitable for plain fabrics and patterns without an obvious design as it interrupts the pattern.

The topstitched casing method leaves the main drop of fabric uninterrupted and requires less fabric but does involve a double row of stitching across the width of the blind. Make the batten casing but do not insert the batten until the lower edge is complete.

When planning a shaped edge, do not be tempted to draw the shaping directly on to the blind fabric as a mistake in measuring or drawing out could leave an ugly mark. Work out the proportions of the shaping, make up a paper pattern, then draw round this to transfer the exact pattern to the blind fabric.

If you are not confident of being able to draw a curve, you will find a flexible curve a worthwhile investment. This is a length of flexible plastic which is easy to bend into smooth, neat curves and retains its shape until re-positioned.

Preparing materials

Details of measuring up, materials required and basic making up instructions for roller blinds are given on pages 76-79. Add an extra 5cm/2in to the length of fabric to cut for a blind with a shaped edge.

Attach the brackets of the roller blind kit to the window and trim the wooden roller to fit. Cut the fabric 1cm/½in narrower than the roller and zigzag the edges to prevent fraying, if necessary.

A stiffened material called Pelmform, described on page 55, has a variety of shapes printed on it for use when making pelmets some of which are also suitable for decorative blind edges.

Making a scalloped blind

This method is also suitable for blinds edged with inverted scallops, zig-zags and wave shapes.

Prepare and cut out the fabric then make a batten casing following one of the two methods below. The blind will only roll up as far as the batten so adjust the depth of scallop to suit the proportions of the window.

The tucked casing is suitable for plain or semi-patterned fabrics. Measure 13cm/5in up from the lower edge of blind fabric and mark on the side edges. Measure 9cm/3½in up from these points and mark again.

Fold the fabric across the width, right sides facing, to bring the two sets of marks together. Finger press the fold (an iron may damage stiffened fabric), then stitch across the width of the fabric 4.5cm/1¾in below the fold (between marks on either side), forming a tuck on the

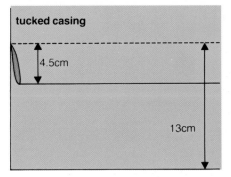

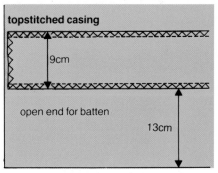

wrong side of the blind. Stitch across one end of the tuck to complete the casing and finger press tuck downwards.

The topstitched casing involves stitching a separate strip of fabric to the wrong side of the blind to form the casing and so does not interrupt the pattern.

Cut a strip 9cm/3½in deep from the bottom edge of the blind and zigzag the edges if they are likely to fray.

Lay the blind fabric wrong side uppermost and position the casing strip, also wrong side up, across the width 13cm/5in up from the lower edge.

Hold in place with adhesive tape or paper clips, as pins may leave permanent marks in the blind. Topstitch down both long edges and across one short edge, leaving the remaining short edge open to insert the batten later.

Planning the scallop pattern

For a scalloped edge (or one with any other repeated shape) to look its best, the width of the scallops has to be carefully calculated so that an exact number fit across the lower edge of the blind. A measurement of between 12cm/4½in and 14cm/5½in at the widest point of each scallop is a reasonable average size but you will be able to judge whether the proportion is correct after making the pattern and laying it against the blind.

To calculate the number of scallops that you need, divide the blind width by an estimated scallop width.

For example, if your blind is 132cm (or imperial equivalent) wide and you would like scallops about 14cm wide, divide 132 by 14. This gives 9.4 as the number of scallops. Obviously, a part scallop looks unbalanced so take the nearest whole number i.e. 9, and divide the width of the blind by this number to give the *exact* width of each scallop. In the example, 132 divided by 9 gives a scallop size of 14.7cm.

Left: Shallow inverted scallops, neatened and defined by a narrow trimming, add interest to a simple blind and echo the shaped edge of a pretty net curtain.

Cutting out the pattern

Cut a strip of paper 13cm/5in deep by the width of your blind and mark it out into sections *half* the calculated scallop width.

Fold the paper *concertina fashion* along the marked sections. On the unfolded edge at one end of the paper, make a mark 6cm/2¼in up from the bottom. Using a flexible curve for absolute accuracy, draw half a scallop curving from the bottom folded corner to the mark. Cut along the curve through all thicknesses of the paper and open the paper out. You will now have a paper pattern of even scallops to fit the width of your blind.

Note: If you are making a wide blind and the bulk of the folded paper is too much to cut through, cut two strips, each exactly half the blind width. Cut each into scallops, and then join the two pieces with adhesive tape to make a pattern to fit the complete blind width.

Shaping the blind edge

Lay the pattern on the wrong side of the blind, with the shaped edge close to the lower edge of the blind, and hold in place with adhesive tape.

With a sharp tailor's chalk pencil, carefully draw round the shaped

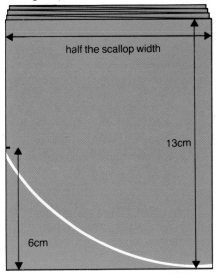

cutting the pattern

edge of the pattern. Remove the pattern and check that the outline is smooth and even.

Cut the fabric along the shaping line with a scalpel, DIY cutting knife or a special rotary cutting wheel (sold as a dressmaking/craft aid). Zigzag stitch around the shaping if it is liable to fray.

Insert the batten into the casing and hand stitch or machine stitch the remaining open edge to close.

Attach the cord holder and cord to the back of the batten, attach the blind to the wooden roller, and hang it at the window.

Shaping variations

Follow the method of making up a scalloped blind, but choose one of the variations below for the shaping.

Inverted scallops

Calculate the width of these and prepare the pattern as for the scallop edged blind.

Having folded the paper concertina fashion to half a scallop width, mark 4cm/1½in (or your required scallop depth) up on the folded edge of the top piece of paper. Draw half an inverted scallop (like a shallow rainbow) from this point to the lower unfolded corner. Cut through all thicknesses and unfold to make the pattern.

Zigzags

Estimate the number and width of zigzags that will fit across the blind, using the same calculation method as for scallops – 10cm/4in wide is an average size. Half the width is a good guide to estimating the height of zigzags, but alter proportions to suit your blind.

Fold a strip of paper concertina fashion to half the width of a zigzag, as for scallops, but mark the top unfolded edge the required

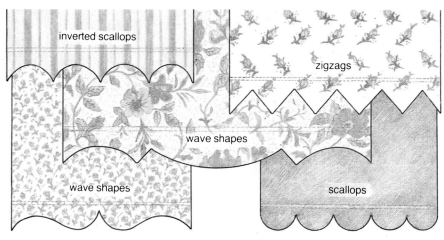

height of zigzag (about 5cm/2in) from the bottom. Rule a straight line from this mark down to the bottom corner on the folded side.

Cut along the line through all layers and unfold to make the pattern.

Wave shapes

These differ from repeated shapes such as scallops and zigzags as one shape covers half the width of the blind and is reversed to cover the other half.

Cut a strip of paper 12cm/4¾in deep by the width of the blind and fold in half, short ends together.

For a deep wave shape, draw a line across the full width of the folded paper 6cm/2¼in up from the bottom edge. For a shallower shape, draw the line about 4cm/1½in up from the bottom edge. Draw two or three evenly spaced vertical lines and use these and the horizontal line as a guide, when you are designing your required shape. A flexible curve makes this easy to do.

Cut out the shape through both layers of paper, unfold and check that the shape is visually pleasing, altering if necessary, before using as the pattern.

Adding a decorative trimming

In addition to, or instead of, cutting the bottom of your blind into a decorative shape, glue a pretty braid trimming – with or without fringing, tassels or bobbles – to the blind edges.

Use any type of braid trim along the bottom of a straight edged roller

blind, but to attach braid around a curved shape, you must use bias cut braid or a flexible woven braid that will bend around the curves without puckering.

If the ends of the braid are liable to fray, either neaten with a zigzag stitch or turn a small amount of braid to the wrong side at each end and glue.

Use a fabric adhesive such as Copydex and follow the manufacturer's instructions to simply glue the braid along the edge of the blind.

A beautiful fabric print, which might be lost in the folds of a curtain, shows to perfection on a roller blind. The elegant wave shaped cut edge increases the stylish effect.

Austrian blinds

A pretty fabric teased into soft swags and gentle gathers makes an Austrian blind a charming alternative, or addition, to curtains. It looks impressively complicated but is easy to make by simply adding tape, rings and cord to an unlined curtain.

An Austrian blind – not to be confused with the ruched festoon blind described in the next chapter – gives a designer look to any room.

When completely lowered it looks like an unlined gathered curtain. The blind is pulled up by cords which are attached to rings and tapes running vertically up the back of the blind. Three types of tape can be used:

Plain woven tape (non-stretch) which has no pockets or bars. Rings have to be sewn on. Buy this about 2cm/¾in wide.

Dainty tape made by Rufflette. A lightweight, narrow curtain heading tape that is ideal for the vertical tapes on Austrian blinds. It has regular pockets for the rings to slot into, which also makes the job of spacing the rings much easier.

Austrian blind tape supplied in Rufflette's Austrian Blind Kit. This tape has regularly spaced bars for holding the cord so rings are not required.

The spacing of the rings and the ac-

Measuring up for an Austrian blind

To calculate how much fabric to buy, first measure your window.

For the width – as a general guide you will need 2-2½ times the window measurement. Check the instructions for the curtain heading tape you are using at the top of the blind, and be sure to allow enough fabric width to form the heading pleats. For all but the narrowest of windows, you will have to use more than one width of fabric.

For the drop – take the window height measurement and allow an extra 20cm/7¾in for hems. Add an allowance for pattern matching the width of fabric, if necessary. Multiply this total drop measurement by the number of fabric widths needed to arrive at the amount of fabric you need.

You will need extra fabric for a frill along the bottom edge, or if you add bows (see Design Extra on page 87).

The amount of tape needed depends on the size of blind you are making – (see above for the types of tape available). The total width of the fabric is divided into sections by vertical lines of tape spaced about 40cm/15¾in apart. You will need sufficient tape to run from top to bottom of the blind along each vertical division and down each side of the blind fabric.

Joining and hemming the fabric

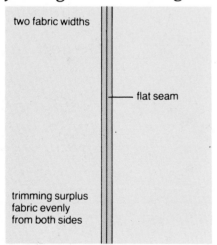

two fabric widths

— flat seam

trimming surplus fabric evenly from both sides

three fabric widths

2cm side hem

2cm side hem

— flat seam

— flat seam

2cm double hem

For most windows you will have to join at least two pieces of fabric to make up the width of the blind.

For two fabric widths Join widths together with a flat seam of 1.5cm/⅝in and then trim seam allowance to 5mm/¼in. Cut any surplus fabric evenly from both widths.

For three fabric widths, position a complete width in the centre, and join the widths together with flat

seams of 1.5cm/⅝in. Trim the seam allowance to 5mm/¼in. Cut any surplus fabric evenly from both side widths. Down each side edge of the blind, turn a 2cm/¾in hem to wrong side and tack in place. Do not make this hem if you are adding side frills. For a plain bottom edge, turn a double hem (2cm and 2cm/¾in and ¾in) to wrong side and sew in place. Do not make this hem if you

are adding a bottom frill.

If you are adding a frill, make up and sew it in place (see Design Extra on page 87).

Right: A prettily trimmed frill emphasises the luxurious festooned effect of an Austrian blind. Piping and binding pick up the print colouring and a row of extravagantly styled bows adds a final flourish.

tion of pulling up the cords raises the blind into swags and gathers which form the characteristic appearance of an Austrian blind.

The swags and gathers raise up from the bottom, so the higher you pull up the blind, the more gathers are formed. Once you have raised the blind into the most visually pleasing position, you keep it in place by securing the cords around a cleat on the window frame.

An Austrian blind can be used at a window in addition to normal curtains, to give an extra soft look. Many people prefer to have both so that the blind can be left in a swagged position for decorative effect and the curtains can be drawn for privacy.

Because of its soft, frilly look, an Austrian blind can be used very effectively to make a feature of a plain window. You can use sheer fabric and most light furnishing fabrics, leaving the blind quite plain or adding a frilled bottom edge – trimmed and piped if you wish. You could also add frills down the side edges, or a set of bows to jolly up the top of the blind.

You will need
Fabric (as calculated opposite)
Matching sewing thread
Wooden batten 2.5cm/1in×5cm/2in ×width of your window
Curtain track and fittings of the same width as the batten
You will also need (unless you have purchased Rufflette's Austrian Blind Kit in which the items *below* are included):
Tape (as calculated opposite)
Small metal curtain rings (also known as split rings)
Non-stretch cord (about double the amount of tape required)
Screw eyes (one per length of tape)
Curtain heading tape to fit the total fabric width
1 cleat

Tapes, rings and cords

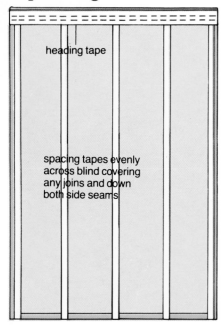

heading tape

spacing tapes evenly across blind covering any joins and down both side seams

Attaching the tapes Wrong sides facing upwards, lay the blind fabric on a large flat surface – the floor is the best place.

With tailor's chalk, mark on the vertical lines for positioning the tape. These must be evenly spaced – about 40cm/16in apart – across the fabric to give good sized swags. If you have joined fabric to make up the complete width, each join must be covered by one of the lengths of tape to disguise the seam. This may mean that you have to adjust the distance between the marked vertical lines slightly – but you must still keep them evenly spaced.

The tape is positioned along these marked lines and also down both outer edges of the blind.

If you are using plain woven tape, cut it into lengths equal to the blind fabric drop plus 1cm/½in. Turn 1cm/½in to wrong side on one end of each tape. Place each length of tape along a marked vertical line (or seamline) with the folded end to the bottom edge of the blind and raw end to the top edge. Place a length of tape down each side of the blind. Tack the tapes in place, then sew down both long edges of the tape.

If you are using Dainty tape or the Austrian blind kit tape, cut each length at exactly the same point on the tape so that when all of the cut lengths are in position the pockets or bars line up across the width. Apply as for the plain tape, ensuring that the pockets or bars face upwards.

Sew heading tape to the top of the blind, as for a curtain, but do not gather up yet.

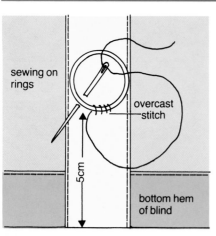

sewing on rings

overcast stitch

5cm

bottom hem of blind

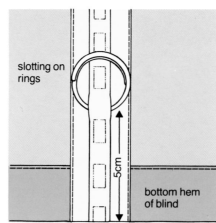

slotting on rings

5cm

bottom hem of blind

Sewn-on rings If you have used plain woven tape on your blind, you will need to sew rings to the tape using overcast stitch. Starting at the bottom left-hand corner, sew the first ring to the tape, placing it 5cm/2in from the bottom edge. Continue up the tape

attaching the rings, spacing them evenly about 20cm/8in apart. Repeat for the other tapes, starting from exactly the same point at the bottom for each one. It's very important to space the rings accurately, because if they do not line up horizontally the blind will not hang evenly.

Slotted-in rings Starting at the bottom left-hand corner, slot a ring through a pocket on the first length of tape, about 5cm/2in from bottom edge. Continue spacing the rings accurately as for the sewn-on rings; you will find them easy to space as you simply count the number of pockets between each ring.

Note: the tape supplied in the Rufflette Austrian blind kit has retaining bars instead of rings. When all the rings are in place, pull up the cords in the heading tape at the top of the blind, gathering up the fabric evenly until it is the correct width for the window.

Cording the blind Lay the blind flat, wrong side upwards. Starting at the bottom left-hand corner, measure the length of the blind, plus the top width plus one metre extra. Cut a piece of cord to this

Hanging the blind

1 Take the batten of wood and fix the curtain track along one of the 5cm/2in sides, close to the top edge. Pull up curtain tape to fit track and insert hooks. Lay the batten on the floor and fit the blind to the curtain track. Turn over so that tape side of blind faces upwards and, with a pencil, mark on the underside of the batten where each tape meets the batten. Remove blind from track.

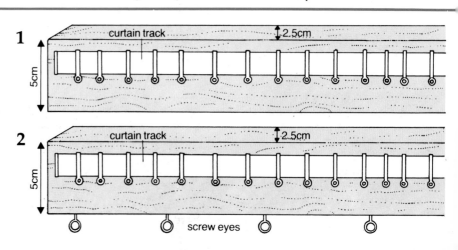

1 curtain track 2.5cm 5cm

2 curtain track 2.5cm 5cm screw eyes

Adding frills and bows

Frills and bows add extra softness and charm to an Austrian blind, and they are easy to make up and attach.

For the frill Cut and join sufficient 10cm/4in wide strips of fabric to make up double the width of the blind. Turn a double hem (5mm and 5mm/¼in and ¼in) to the wrong side along one long edge and both short edges. On remaining long edge, sew two lines of gathering stitches 1cm/½in and 1.5cm/⅝in from the edge. Draw up gathering threads until the frill exactly fits the bottom of the blind.

With right sides facing, tack and then sew raw edges of frill and blind together, with a 1cm/½in flat seam. Insert piping between

frill and blind at this stage if desired. Remove tacking and neaten seam with zigzag or overcasting stitch.

A row of bows are a clever way to conceal the seams in the fabric. For each bow, cut a strip of fabric 70cm×6cm/27½in×2¼in. Fold in half lengthways, wrong sides facing, and cut each end into a point. Trim all edges with bias binding, or bias strips cut from fabric. Tie each fabric strip into a bow. Stitch bows to blind along gathered heading.

Right: Designer touches give a really professional finish to an Austrian blind. Piped seams, a flouncy frill, contrasting binding or a row of bows – choose one or add them all for maximum effect.

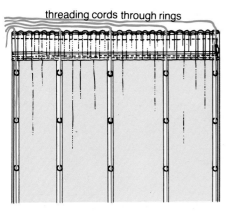

threading cords through rings

measurement.

Tie this first cord in place to the bottom ring, or bottom bar, of the tape in the bottom left-hand corner and thread it up through the other rings/bars.

Add cords to the other tape lengths in the same way, working across to the right-hand side of the blind.

2 Fix a screw eye in place on each pencil mark along the batten. Screw each end of the batten to the window frame.

Hang the blind on the curtain track.
3 Thread the left-hand cord through the first screw eye and then through all the screw eyes to the right-hand side of the batten.

Repeat for the other cords.

Attach the cleat about half-way down the right-hand side of the window frame.

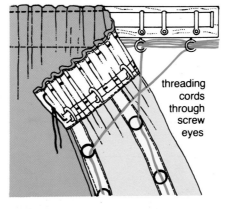

threading cords through screw eyes

Above: In a sheer fabric, an Austrian blind lets in softly filtered light.

To check that the blind pulls up properly, pull the cords evenly together, so that the fabric gathers upwards into soft swags.

Lower the blind, so that it is flat and tie the cords together in a knot, trimming ends to make a neat bunch. Pull the blind up once more, until it is in the desired position and secure the cords around the cleat.

87

Elegantly ruched festoon blinds

Even more sumptuous than an Austrian blind, a festoon blind remains ruched into soft swags not only when pulled up but also when fully covering the window. Emphasize the pretty scalloped effect of the lower edge with a matching or contrasting frill.

Transform a dull window by making a strikingly decorative ruched festoon blind, highlighting the scallops of the lower edge with a deep gathered frill. Choose a richly printed furnishing fabric, or use a sheer voile for a translucent blind to team with heavier side curtains.

A festoon blind is very similar to an Austrian blind but retains the ruched swags whether raised or lowered and so creates an even more dramatic effect. Read the previous chapter on making Austrian blinds and adapt, as described here, to make a festoon blind. Vertical lines of curtain tape – lightweight Dainty Tape is ideal – gather up the extra length.

A rod or batten encased in matching fabric, stitched to the back of the blind, ensures that the bottom edge hangs well and is easy to raise and lower smoothly. Choose a metal rod about 1cm/½in in diameter or, adding curtain weighting tape to increase the weight if necessary, a wooden batten about 2cm/¾in deep.

Below: Piping and a frill add to the decorative effect of a festoon blind.

You will need

Fabric for the blind, frill and batten casing (see Measuring up)
Rufflette Dainty tape for vertical tapes (see Measuring up)
Blind cord about twice length of tape
Rufflette Standard curtain heading tape to fit width of prepared blind fabric plus turnings
Small split curtain rings
Screw eyes
Metal rod or wooden batten to fit finished blind width
Wooden heading batten, curtain track and hooks to hang blind
Cleat to hold cords
Note: The tape in an Austrian blind kit does not create permanent ruching.

Measuring up

To calculate how much fabric to buy, measure the width and drop of your window (or the area to be covered by the finished blind).
Multiply the width by 1¼ times for a medium-weight fabric or by 1½ times for lightweights and sheers, to find the width of fabric needed. You may need more than one width of fabric to make up this size.
Multiply the drop by 1½-3 times (again, the bulkier the fabric, the less you need; only a fine sheer needs 3 times the drop) to find the required length of blind fabric.
Calculate how much fabric you will need to buy by multiplying the required length by the number of widths needed. You will also need sufficient 20cm/8in-deep strips of fabric to make up a piece 1½ times the width of prepared blind fabric for the frill and a strip of fabric 8cm/3in deep by the width of the finished blind to cover the rod or batten.
Add allowances for pattern matching as necessary.
Calculate the Dainty tape needed as for an Austrian blind, page 84.

Cutting out

Allowing for pattern matching where necessary, cut out lengths of fabric to make up the area of the blind. Also cut 20cm/8in deep strips to make up a frill piece 1½ times the blind fabric width, and a strip for batten casing (see Measuring up).

Making up and hanging the blind

Join widths of fabric if necessary, as for an Austrian blind, page 84.
Press a 2cm/¾in turning to the wrong side down each side edge of the blind and tack.
Press a 4cm/1½in turning to the wrong side across the top edge; tack.

Adding the frill

Join the strips of fabric to make up the frill with 1cm/½in flat seams and press seams open. Fold the strip in half along its length, right sides facing, and stitch across both short ends, 1cm/½in in. Fold strip right side out, press and insert two rows of gathering stitches, in easy-to-gather sections, through both thicknesses along the open edge. Pull up the gathering threads until the frill fits the width of the blind, tie the thread ends securely and even out gathers.
Tack the frill across the bottom edge on the right side of the blind, raw edges together, and stitch 1.5cm/⅝in in from the edge. Remove tacking, zigzag stitch or oversew raw edges together; press upwards.

Attaching tapes and rings

Lay the fabric out flat on the floor, wrong side uppermost and, using a tailor's chalk pencil, mark the position of the vertical lines of Dainty tape. Position the two outer tapes 1cm/½in in from the side edges; space the remaining tapes evenly between them 25–40cm/10–16in apart. If possible, arrange the

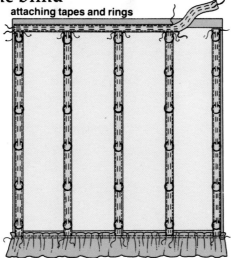
attaching tapes and rings

spacing so that a line of tape will cover any seams joining fabric widths. Cutting 1cm/½in in front of a tape pocket each time, so that they will line up horizontally on the blind, cut the appropriate number of lengths of tape each 5cm/2in longer than blind (excluding frill). Freeing the ends of the gathering cords, turn in 1cm/½in at the lower end of each length of tape, and pin into position from the frill seam to the edge of top turning. Ensure that the edges of the side hems and any seams are covered by tape and that the tape pockets line up. Stitch long edges of each tape.
Freeing the top ends of gathering cords on vertical tapes as shown in diagram, stitch standard heading tape across top of blind covering raw edge and tape ends.
Slot split rings through the tape pockets every 20–25cm/8–10in or so, placing the first ring about 10cm/4in up from the bottom of the tape, with the final ring just below the heading tape.
Gather up each line of tape to the finished length of the blind. Even out the gathering so that the rings line up horizontally across the back of the blind and tie the ends of the cords to secure. Just below each pocket, catch the cords of the gathering tape to the fabric with small invisible handstitches to hold the gathers in place as heavy fabrics may slip when hanging.

Adding a rod or batten

Fold the strip of casing fabric in half lengthwise, right sides facing, and stitch across one short end and down long raw edges with a 1cm/½in seam. Turn right side out.
Slip the rod, or a batten plus weighting tape, into the casing and slipstitch the open end closed.
Lay the blind out flat, wrong side upwards and place the covered rod just below the lowest row of rings as close to the scallops as possible without being visible from the right side. Stitch the top edge of the casing securely in place at the points where it crosses the vertical tapes, making sure the stitches are unnoticeable on the right side.

Cording and hanging

Attach cords and hang the blind in the same way as an Austrian blind.

Roman blinds for a soft pleated effect

Softer than a roller blind and less fussy than an Austrian blind, a Roman blind suits most windows and rooms, and is quick and economical to make. It is also easy to hang and to operate – the pull cords which raise it form attractive layered folds.

A Roman blind is an economical and unusual way of covering a window. When fully lowered it looks similar to a roller blind, but when pulled up, a system of rings and cords on the back concertina the fabric into soft horizontal pleats. There is, therefore, no need to stiffen the fabric, or buy a spring-loaded roller blind kit. A wooden batten running across the blind close to the bottom edge keeps it in shape and hanging straight.

Choosing fabrics

A Roman blind is made from a double thickness of fabric – top blind fabric and lining. The top fabric must not be too sheer or flimsy or it will not fall into crisp pleats. Most smoothly woven furnishing fabrics are suitable – choose one to match your upholstery or the colour scheme of the room. The lining can be ordinary curtain lining, an insulating lining or a complementary fabric that will also look pretty from the outside of the house. Choose closely woven fabrics for both blind and lining and the blind will be light-tight enough even for a bedroom.

The blind is quick and simple to make. After joining fabric and lining, simply stitch vertical lines of tape down its length. Sew rings to the tapes and pass cords through them – when pulled, the cords raise the blind by pleating up the fabric.

Tack the blind to a length of wood for hanging, and fix it to the wall with small angle iron supports, available from most hardwear or DIY suppliers.

Measuring up

The width Measure the width of the window area to be covered by the

Below: An elegant set of Roman blinds.

blind. If the blind is to be hung inside a recess or within a decorative window frame, make sure that the finished width will allow enough clearance for the blind to be raised and lowered without catching on the sides. If the blind is to hang outside a recess, overlap each side by at least 3cm/1¼in. For either style of hanging, add 3cm/1¼in to the finished width measurement for side seams.

It is possible to make a blind for a smallish window from a single piece of fabric. If you do have to join widths of fabric for a larger window, balance the joins evenly – for two widths the join should run down the exact centre of the blind; for three widths, use a complete width for the centre panel with an equal amount of fabric on either side.

For each join required, add 3cm/1¼in to make a 1.5cm/⅝in flat seam.

The length Measure the total drop required and add 3cm/1¼in for top and bottom seams and 1cm/½in for

overlapping the blind fabric on to the wooden heading. If you are hanging the blind outside a recess, add any overlap required at the top or bottom.

The tape Calculate the amount needed in the same way as for an Austrian blind (see page 84).

The finished width of the blind is divided into equal sections by vertical lines of tape spaced at approximately 30cm/12in intervals across the width – with a length of tape on each side edge. To work out the amount of tape required, calculate the number of lengths of tape needed and multiply this by the finished length of the blind plus 2cm/¾in.

You will need
To make the blind
Fabric for the front of the blind (see measuring up)
The same amount of lining fabric
Matching sewing thread
2cm/¾in wide cotton tape (see measuring up)

Non-stretch cord about twice the length of tape
Small plastic or metal curtain rings
Wooden batten about 2cm/¾in wide 1cm/½in shorter than finished width of blind

To hang the blind
A piece of 5cm×2.5cm/2in×1in wood to fit the finished width of blind, for the heading
A metal screw eye for each vertical line of tape
Tacks or staples to attach blind to wooden heading
Angle irons to attach wooden heading to window frame
Cleat to hold cords in place

Cutting out
Cut the fabric to the required length and join widths, if necessary, with 1.5cm/⅝in flat seams. Press seams open. Trim away any excess width taking an even amount from each side. Cut out and make up lining to the same size.

Making up the Roman blind

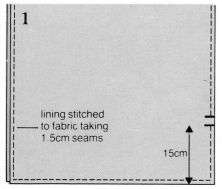

lining stitched to fabric taking 1.5cm seams

15cm

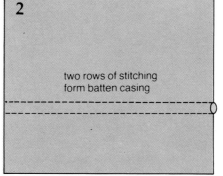

two rows of stitching form batten casing

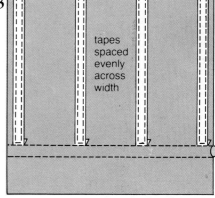

tapes spaced evenly across width

Joining fabric and lining Lay the lining fabric wrong side upwards flat on a table or the floor and measure 15cm/6in up from the bottom on one side edge. Mark this point with tailor's chalk.

Measure the wooden batten, add 5mm/¼in to the width and make a second mark on the lining this distance above the first.

1 Lay fabric and lining right sides facing and tack together all round. Sew down both sides and across the bottom edge taking 1.5cm/⅝in seams leaving a gap between the two marks on *one* side of the fabric to insert batten. Turn right side out. Turn 1.5cm/⅝in to the wrong side on both fabric and lining top edges and press. Tack and topstitch the folded edges together close to edge.

2 Lay the fabric out flat with the lining uppermost. With a ruler and tailor's chalk, mark two parallel lines for the batten casing in line with the gap left in the stitching on one side. Sew along these marked lines to form the batten casing.

Attaching tape and rings Mark the position of the vertical tapes on the lining side of the blind by drawing lines with tailor's chalk from the top of the blind to the batten casing. Begin by marking the position of a line of tape 1.5cm/⅝in in from each side edge. Divide the remaining fabric into equal sections with lines for tapes spaced about 30cm/12in apart, adjusting the spacing to suit your blind depth. It is *vital* that the tapes are evenly spaced.

3 Once you have marked the tape lines and checked that the spacing is even, pin and tack the tapes in place, turning 1cm/½in to the wrong side at the top and bottom ends. The tapes should run from the top edge ending at, but not overlapping, the batten casing. Sew the tapes in place, down both long edges and across the bottom edge. Remove tacking.

With tailor's chalk or pins, mark the ring positions about 15cm/6in apart along each line of tape. The first mark should be just above the batten casing and the last approximately 18.5cm/7in down from the top edge of the blind. It is important that the rings are *exactly* aligned horizontally so that the blind pulls up evenly.

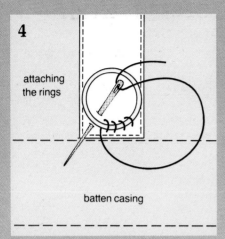

4

attaching the rings

batten casing

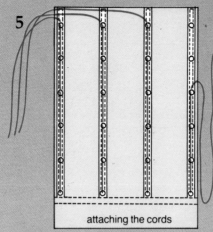

attaching the cords

4 Sew on a ring at each mark, using overcast stitching worked through the tape and lining but not the top blind fabric.

Adding batten and cords Check that the length of wooden batten is 1cm/½in less than the width of the blind; trim it if necessary. Gently

ease it into the stitched casing and neatly hand sew the casing closed.
5 To attach the cords, lay the blind flat on the floor, lining side upwards and tie a length of cord securely to the bottom ring on the left-hand side. Pass the cord through every ring in this first line of tape and across to the left-hand edge of the lining. Allow 1m/1yd or a length that you will be able to reach when the blind is hanging, and then cut the cord.
Repeat for each line of tape, taking the cord up to the top of the blind, across to the left-hand edge and adding approximately 1m/1yd extra before cutting to form the hanging cords which are pulled to operate the blind.

Hanging the Roman blind

Preparing the wooden heading Cut the 5cm×2.5cm/2in×1in piece of wood for the heading to the width of the blind and attach the screw eyes to a wider side, positioning them to correspond with the lines of tape on the blind.
Screw as many angle irons as are necessary to support the blind to the same side of the wood as the screw eyes, placing the bend of the angle iron in line with the edge of the wood.

Below: Use Rufflette Austrian blind tape rather than tape and rings, and thread the cords through the loops.

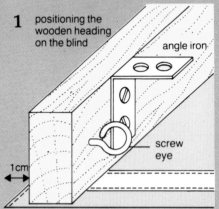

1

positioning the wooden heading on the blind

angle iron

screw eye

1cm

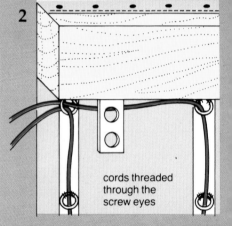

2

cords threaded through the screw eyes

1 With the blind flat on the floor, lining side upwards, lay the narrow edge of the wooden heading (angle irons uppermost), on to the fabric 1cm/½in down from the top edge. Wrap the 1cm/½in strip of blind fabric on the wider side of the wood without screw eyes and tack or staple it securely in place. Make sure that the strip of fabric turned on to the wood is absolutely straight and even or the blind will hang askew.

2 Thread the left-hand vertical cord through the screw eye above it so that it hangs on the left side of the blind. Work across the blind threading each cord through the screw eye directly above and through the other screws along the wood to the left-hand side. When all cords have been inserted loosely knot the dangling ends together. Hold the wood and blind up to the window in the required position and attach the angle irons to the window frame or wall.
Untie the cords and trim to an even length of about 1m/1yd (or as required) then re-tie neatly together.
Pull the bunch of cords downwards and the blind above the batten will pull up in even folds, from the bottom upwards.
Screw a cleat to the window frame in a position within easy reach; wind the cords around this to hold the blind up at the required level.

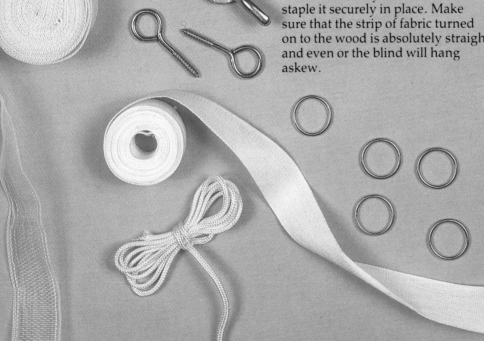

Trimming a Roman blind

Emphasize the neat, clean lines of a Roman blind with a sharply contrasting trim.

Use a flat tape or straight strips of fabric with raw edges pressed under for the trim. A width of 2.5cm/1in wide gives a bold effect.

Make up the blind as far as attaching the tapes to the lining side. Add the trim before attaching the rings.

Lay the blind out flat, right side upwards, and tack the trim in place down both sides and across the bottom edge, mitring the corners. Set the trim about 1.5cm/⅝in in from the edge so that the blind fabric forms a narrow border.

Machine the trim in place, topstitching down both edges, but do not machine over the batten casing. Remove the

Above: On a border-printed fabric, adjust width by making a tuck and only trim lower edge of the blind.

tacking and back stitch by hand along the trim where it crosses the casing, stitching through the top layer of fabric only, so as not to obstruct it.

Press well, sew on the rings and continue to make up the blind in the normal way.

Furnishing fabric guide

Cushions

Almost any fabric can be used, from heavy tapestry weaves to lightweight cottons; the limiting factor is the amount of wear the cushion is likely to get. Avoid very loose weaves and choose fabrics with easy care or washable properties for cushions which will get a lot of use. Remnant counters are a good source of some luxurious fabrics if only a small amount is required. For a co-ordinated look, save offcuts from your curtains and upholstery. Ready-made cushion pads are available but if you intend making your own, suitable fabrics are calico, cambric, cotton sheeting and lining material. If the filling is feather or down, use a down-proof ticking.

Curtains

Traditional curtain fabrics are brocade, velvet, linen and cotton and nowadays there is a wide range of man-made fabrics developed for use in soft furnishing. Some manufacturers produce a range of matching or co-ordinating wallpapers and fabrics, the latter often in two weights suitable for curtains and upholstery. Do not confine yourself to the furnishing-fabric departments – many dressmaking fabrics can also be used successfully for curtains.

Acetate
Man-made fibre made into silky-looking fabrics, often combined with cotton or linen in brocades and open-weave effects. Drapes well but is not very strong. Usually washable; does not shrink.

Acrylic
Synthetic fibre used for lightweight yet strong and crease-resistant fabrics such as velvet and satin. Washable but some varieties may need drycleaning.

Balloon fabrics
A very closely-woven cotton fabric used for cushion interlinings as it is downproof.

Brocade
A heavy fabric with the pattern woven in using a jacquard weave. Cotton, linen or silk is woven with, for example, rayon or acetate to produce a silky pattern on a dull background, or vice versa. Used for curtains.

Buckram
A loosely-woven cotton or linen fabric which is stiffened with glue size. It will not remain stiff if washed. Used for curtain pelmets and tiebacks.

Calico
A hard-wearing, medium-weight plain weave cotton fabric which is often used for cushion interlinings.

Cambric
A lightweight plain weave cotton or linen fabric used as a backing fabric or for lightweight curtains.

Casement cloth
A medium-weight cotton fabric in a closely-woven plain weave dyed in plain colours and used for lightweight curtains and blinds.

Chintz
A printed cotton fabric with a glazed finish. The glaze can be treated chemically to withstand washing. Used for curtains, blinds and cushion covers.

Cotton
Natural fibre which is strong and wears well. Used for many types of fabric, including glazed cotton, which has a shiny finish and resists dirt. Other varieties include velveteen, cotton satin, sateen and towelling. Washable.

Cretonne
A firm plain weave cotton fabric often printed with patterns which have a shadowy outline. It can be reversible and is used for curtains, blinds and cushion covers.

Fibreglass
Man-made fibre which is flame-resistant. Dryclean.

Folkweave
A loosely-woven soft fabric made from a coarse cotton yarn. Often printed with a striped pattern but the colours have a tendency to run if washed. Used for curtains.

Hessian
Made from jute, a natural fibre, it is cheap and comes in a wide range of colours. The loose weave may droop. Dryclean. Used for curtains.

Lace
Synthetic or cotton lace with an all-over pattern is used for lightweight curtains.

Lawn
A sheer, lightweight smooth-woven fabric made from cotton or linen which can be blended with man-made fibres. Use for cushion interlinings or lightweight curtains.

Linen
A plain weave with uneven surface texture made from natural fibre which can be blended with man-made fibres. Used for curtains and blinds.

Milium
Man-made fibre for aluminium-backed curtain lining with good insulation properties. Available in silver, white and cream. Dryclean.

Moiré
Watermark-patterned fabric which gives a waved effect. A fairly stiff, shiny fabric made from silk and from rayon and other man-made fibres. Used for all soft furnishings.

Nylon
Synthetic fibre used for fabrics of all weights and types. Varieties include nylon velvet and nets. Can fade, and may discolour in sunlight. Washable.

Polyester
Synthetic fibre often blended with natural fibres – does not shrink or fade. Drapes well, very strong and used for its sheer and opaque qualities.

The main requirements when choosing fabric are that it drapes well, has stable colours and will not fade excessively in sunlight, wears well and will not shrink or stretch when washed or hung. The fabric label should guide you on these points but, if in doubt, consult the sales assistant. Check whether the fabric is washable or needs to be drycleaned as this will affect your choice of lining and interlining.

Blinds

Closely-woven fabrics which do not have a tendency to fray are most suitable for roller blinds. Lightweight or flimsy fabrics will crease on the roller unless they are dipped, painted or sprayed with fabric stiffener. This has the added advantage of allowing the fabric to be sponged clean. Pvc or pvc-coated fabrics are particularly suitable for bathrooms or kitchens as long as they are not too heavy and bulky fabrics in general should be avoided as they will not roll up successfully.

Some soft-furnishing departments sell made-to-measure roller blind fabric which is spongeable, fade-resistant and does not fray. The patterns are designed specifically for use on a blind.

Austrian and ruched festoon blinds should be made up in a fabric which drapes well and which is not too stiff to gather up in swags across the width. Suitable fabrics include moiré, soft cottons, slubbed satin, dupion and sheer voile.

Roman blinds must be lined and an aluminium-backed lining such as Milium will give added insulation. Choose a firm, closely-woven fabric such as linen-look types or chintz. The fabric must not be too stiff or the blind will not fall in even pleats.

Pvc
A non-porous finish made from polyvinylchloride and applied to woven or knitted base fabrics. Used to make kitchen or bathroom blinds.

Rayon
Also known as viscose. Man-made fibre used in taffeta, linen-look types and velvet. Drapes and wears well but tends to fray so care needed when making up. Hand wash.

Ripstop nylon
A lightweight man-made fabric which comes in a range of bright colours. Used for shower curtains.

Sateen
A strong lightweight cotton fabric which has a sheen on one side. Often used for curtain linings.

Satin
A special weave in which threads 'float' over the base threads to give a surface sheen. Made from silk, rayon or man-made fibres and used for curtains and cushion covers.

Silk
Natural fibre fabric in all weights and types. May fade in bright sunlight. Dryclean or hand wash with care.

Ticking
A closely-woven, strong cotton or linen fabric, often with a characteristic stripe. Used for cushion interlinings.

Velvet
A warp-pile fabric made from silk, cotton or man-made fibres. Used for curtains.

Velveteen
A short, closely-set piled fabric on a cotton base. The heavier weights are suitable for curtains.

Viscose
See Rayon

Standard aftercare symbols

 A tub indicates that the yarn can be hand or machine washed.

 A hand in the tub means hand wash only.

 A figure in the water shows the correct water temperature. Numbers 1 to 9 above the water line denote washing machine programmes.

 Where the tub is crossed through, dry-clean only.

 An iron means the yarn can be pressed – one dot means cool; two dots medium and three dots hot.

 Where the iron is crossed through do not attempt to press the yarn or you may ruin the fabric.

 An empty circle means the yarn can be dry-cleaned.

 An A inside the circle means dry-cleaning in all solvents.

 The letter P means dry-cleaning only in certain solvents.

 The letter F means dry-cleaning only in certain solvents.

 Where the circle is crossed through do *not* dry-clean.

 A triangle means that the yarn can be bleached.

 Where the triangle is crossed through do not bleach.

 Square signs denote drying instructions.

 Three vertical lines in a square means drip dry.

 One horizontal line in a square means dry flat.

 A circle in a square means tumble dry.

 A loop at the top of a square means dry on a line.

Index